CONNECTED MATHEMATICS 3

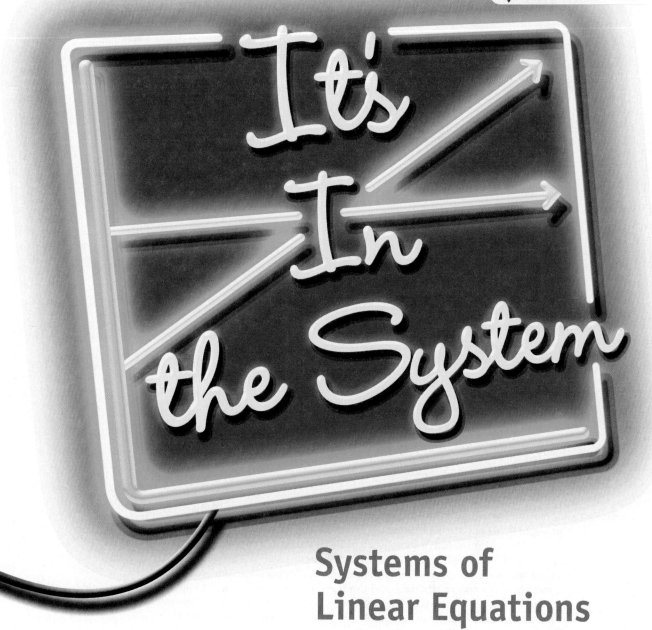

It's In the System

Systems of Linear Equations and Inequalities

Glenda Lappan, Elizabeth Difanis Phillips, James T. Fey, Susan N. Friel

Pearson

Boston, Massachusetts

Connected Mathematics® was developed at Michigan State University with financial support from the Michigan State University Office of the Provost, Computing and Technology, and the College of Natural Science.

 This material is based upon work supported by the National Science Foundation under Grant No. MDR 9150217 and Grant No. ESI 9986372. Opinions expressed are those of the authors and not necessarily those of the Foundation.

As with prior editions of this work, the authors and administration of Michigan State University preserve a tradition of devoting royalties from this publication to support activities sponsored by the MSU Mathematics Education Enrichment Fund.

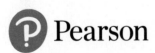

13-digit ISBN 978-0-328-90059-6
10-digit ISBN 0-328-90059-1
1 17

Authors

A Team of Experts

Glenda Lappan is a University Distinguished Professor in the Program in Mathematics Education (PRIME) and the Department of Mathematics at Michigan State University. Her research and development interests are in the connected areas of students' learning of mathematics and mathematics teachers' professional growth and change related to the development and enactment of K–12 curriculum materials.

Elizabeth Difanis Phillips is a Senior Academic Specialist in the Program in Mathematics Education (PRIME) and the Department of Mathematics at Michigan State University. She is interested in teaching and learning mathematics for both teachers and students. These interests have led to curriculum and professional development projects at the middle school and high school levels, as well as projects related to the teaching and learning of algebra across the grades.

James T. Fey is a Professor Emeritus at the University of Maryland. His consistent professional interest has been development and research focused on curriculum materials that engage middle and high school students in problem-based collaborative investigations of mathematical ideas and their applications.

Susan N. Friel is a Professor of Mathematics Education in the School of Education at the University of North Carolina at Chapel Hill. Her research interests focus on statistics education for middle-grade students and, more broadly, on teachers' professional development and growth in teaching mathematics K–8.

With... Yvonne Grant and Jacqueline Stewart

Yvonne Grant teaches mathematics at Portland Middle School in Portland, Michigan. Jacqueline Stewart is a recently retired high school teacher of mathematics at Okemos High School in Okemos, Michigan. Both Yvonne and Jacqueline have worked on a variety of activities related to the development, implementation, and professional development of the CMP curriculum since its beginning in 1991.

Development Team

CMP3 Authors

Glenda Lappan, University Distinguished Professor, Michigan State University
Elizabeth Difanis Phillips, Senior Academic Specialist, Michigan State University
James T. Fey, Professor Emeritus, University of Maryland
Susan N. Friel, Professor, University of North Carolina – Chapel Hill

With...
Yvonne Grant, Portland Middle School, Michigan
Jacqueline Stewart, Mathematics Consultant, Mason, Michigan

In Memory of... William M. Fitzgerald, Professor (Deceased), Michigan State University, who made substantial contributions to conceptualizing and creating CMP1.

Administrative Assistant

Michigan State University
Judith Martus Miller

Support Staff

Michigan State University
Undergraduate Assistants:
Bradley Robert Corlett, Carly Fleming, Erin Lucian, Scooter Nowak

Development Assistants

Michigan State University
Graduate Research Assistants:
Richard "Abe" Edwards, Nic Gilbertson, Funda Gonulates, Aladar Horvath, Eun Mi Kim, Kevin Lawrence, Jennifer Nimtz, Joanne Philhower, Sasha Wang

Assessment Team

Maine
Falmouth Public Schools
Falmouth Middle School: Shawn Towle

Michigan
Ann Arbor Public Schools
Tappan Middle School
Anne Marie Nicoll-Turner
Portland Public Schools
Portland Middle School
Holly DeRosia, Yvonne Grant
Traverse City Area Public Schools
Traverse City East Middle School
Jane Porath, Mary Beth Schmitt

Traverse City West Middle School
Jennifer Rundio, Karrie Tufts

Ohio
Clark-Shawnee Local Schools
Rockway Middle School: Jim Mamer

Content Consultants

Michigan State University
Peter Lappan, Professor Emeritus, Department of Mathematics

Normandale Community College
Christopher Danielson, Instructor, Department of Mathematics & Statistics

University of North Carolina – Wilmington
Dargan Frierson, Jr., Professor, Department of Mathematics & Statistics

Student Activities
Michigan State University
Brin Keller, Associate Professor, Department of Mathematics

Consultants

Indiana
Purdue University
Mary Bouck, Mathematics Consultant

Michigan
Oakland Schools
Valerie Mills, Mathematics Education
Supervisor
Mathematics Education Consultants:
Geraldine Devine, Dana Gosen

Ellen Bacon, Independent Mathematics
Consultant

New York
University of Rochester
Jeffrey Choppin, Associate Professor

Ohio
University of Toledo
Debra Johanning, Associate Professor

Pennsylvania
University of Pittsburgh
Margaret Smith, Professor

Texas
University of Texas at Austin
Emma Trevino, Supervisor of
Mathematics Programs, The Dana Center

Mathematics for All Consulting
Carmen Whitman, Mathematics Consultant

....

Reviewers

Michigan
Ionia Public Schools
Kathy Dole, Director of Curriculum
and Instruction

Grand Valley State University
Lisa Kasmer, Assistant Professor

Portland Public Schools
Teri Keusch, Classroom Teacher

Minnesota
Hopkins School District 270
Michele Luke, Mathematics Coordinator

....

Field Test Sites for CMP3

Michigan
Ann Arbor Public Schools
Tappan Middle School
Anne Marie Nicoll-Turner*

Portland Public Schools
Portland Middle School: Mark Braun,
Angela Buckland, Holly DeRosia,
Holly Feldpausch, Angela Foote,
Yvonne Grant*, Kristin Roberts,
Angie Stump, Tammi Wardwell

Traverse City Area Public Schools
Traverse City East Middle School
Ivanka Baic Berkshire, Brenda Dunscombe,
Tracie Herzberg, Deb Larimer, Jan Palkowski,
Rebecca Perreault, Jane Porath*,
Robert Sagan, Mary Beth Schmitt*

Traverse City West Middle School
Pamela Alfieri, Jennifer Rundio,
Maria Taplin, Karrie Tufts*

Maine
Falmouth Public Schools
Falmouth Middle School: Sally Bennett,
Chris Driscoll, Sara Jones, Shawn Towle*

Minnesota
Minneapolis Public Schools
Jefferson Community School
Leif Carlson*,
Katrina Hayek Munsisoumang*

Ohio
Clark-Shawnee Local Schools
Reid School: Joanne Gilley
Rockway Middle School: Jim Mamer*
Possum School: Tami Thomas

*Indicates a Field Test Site Coordinator

It's In the System

Systems of Linear Equations and Inequalities

1 Linear Equations With Two Variables   7

2 Solving Linear Systems Symbolically   24

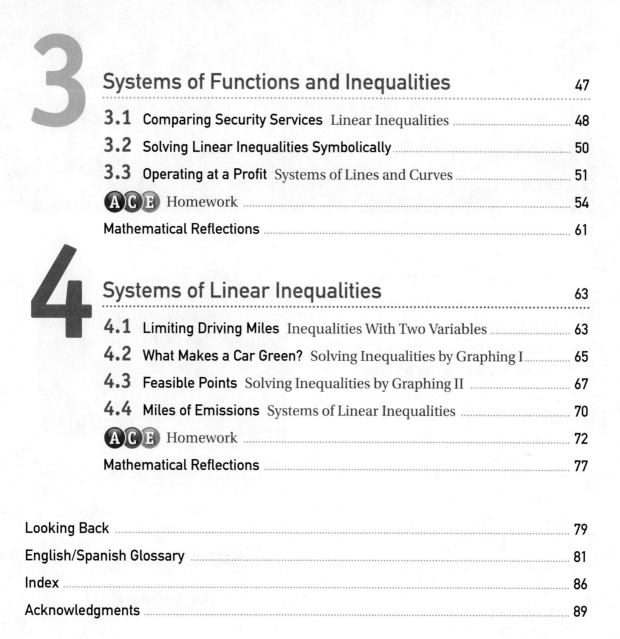

Looking Ahead

Pablo, Jasmine, and their brothers visit a taco truck for lunch. Pablo and his brother order 6 tacos and 2 drinks for $9. Jasmine and her brother order 4 tacos and 2 drinks for $7. **What** is the price of one taco and the price of one drink?

The owners of a shopping center get bids from two security companies. Super Locks charges $3,975 plus $6 per day. Fail Safe charges $995 plus $17.95 per day. For **what** number of days will Super Locks cost less than Fail Safe?

A family wants to drive their car and SUV at most 1,000 miles each month. **What** are some pairs (*car miles, SUV miles*) that meet this condition?

In this Unit, you will apply and extend what you have learned about the properties of equality, linear equations, and methods for solving equations and inequalities. You will learn graphic and symbolic methods for solving systems of linear equations and inequalities. As you work in this Unit, you will solve problems about admission fees for various events, as well as those on the previous page.

Mathematical Highlights

In this Unit, you will write and solve systems of linear equations and inequalities that model real-world situations. The methods for solving these algebraic systems combine graphic and algebraic reasoning from earlier *Connected Mathematics* Units.

You will learn how to

- Solve linear equations and systems of linear equations with two variables

- Solve linear inequalities and systems of inequalities with two variables

- Use systems of linear equations and inequalities to solve problems

When you encounter a new problem, it is a good idea to ask yourself questions. In this Unit, you might ask questions such as:

What are the variables in this problem?

Does the problem call for solving a system of equations or inequalities relating those variables?

What strategy will be most effective in solving the system?

Mathematical Practices and Habits of Mind

In the *Connected Mathematics* curriculum you will develop an understanding of important mathematical ideas by solving problems and reflecting on the mathematics involved. Every day, you will use "habits of mind" to make sense of problems and apply what you learn to new situations. Some of these habits are described by the *Common Core State Standards for Mathematical Practices* (MP).

MP1 Make sense of problems and persevere in solving them.

When using mathematics to solve a problem, it helps to think carefully about

- data and other facts you are given and what additional information you need to solve the problem;
- strategies you have used to solve similar problems and whether you could solve a related simpler problem first;
- how you could express the problem with equations, diagrams, or graphs;
- whether your answer makes sense.

MP2 Reason abstractly and quantitatively.

When you are asked to solve a problem, it often helps to

- focus first on the key mathematical ideas;
- check that your answer makes sense in the problem setting;
- use what you know about the problem setting to guide your mathematical reasoning.

MP3 Construct viable arguments and critique the reasoning of others.

When you are asked to explain why a conjecture is correct, you can

- show some examples that fit the claim and explain why they fit;
- show how a new result follows logically from known facts and principles.

When you believe a mathematical claim is incorrect, you can

- show one or more counterexamples—cases that don't fit the claim;
- find steps in the argument that do not follow logically from prior claims.

MP4 Model with mathematics.

When you are asked to solve problems, it often helps to

- think carefully about the numbers or geometric shapes that are the most important factors in the problem, then ask yourself how those factors are related to each other;
- express data and relationships in the problem with tables, graphs, diagrams, or equations, and check your result to see if it makes sense.

MP5 Use appropriate tools strategically.

When working on mathematical questions, you should always

- decide which tools are most helpful for solving the problem and why;
- try a different tool when you get stuck.

MP6 Attend to precision.

In every mathematical exploration or problem-solving task, it is important to

- think carefully about the required accuracy of results; is a number estimate or geometric sketch good enough, or is a precise value or drawing needed?
- report your discoveries with clear and correct mathematical language that can be understood by those to whom you are speaking or writing.

MP7 Look for and make use of structure.

In mathematical explorations and problem solving, it is often helpful to

- look for patterns that show how data points, numbers, or geometric shapes are related to each other;
- use patterns to make predictions.

MP8 Look for and express regularity in repeated reasoning.

When results of a repeated calculation show a pattern, it helps to

- express that pattern as a general rule that can be used in similar cases;
- look for shortcuts that will make the calculation simpler in other cases.

You will use all of the Mathematical Practices in this Unit. Sometimes, when you look at a Problem, it is obvious which practice is most helpful. At other times, you will decide on a practice to use during class explorations and discussions. After completing each Problem, ask yourself:

- What mathematics have I learned by solving this Problem?
- What Mathematical Practices were helpful in learning this mathematics?

Linear Equations With Two Variables

Solving equations is one of the most common and useful tasks in mathematics. In earlier Units, you learned how to solve

- linear equations, such as $3x + 5 = 17$.

- proportions, such as $\frac{3}{5} = \frac{6}{x}$.

- quadratic equations, such as $x^2 - 5x + 6 = 0$.

- exponential equations, such as $2^{x+1} = 64$.

The Problems of this Investigation pose a new challenge. You will learn to solve linear equations, such as $3x + 5y = 11$, that have two variables.

- What does a solution for this equation look like?

- What does a graph of this equation look like?

Common Core State Standards

8.EE.C.8 Analyze and solve pairs of simultaneous linear equations.

8.EE.C.8a Understand that solutions to a system of two linear equations in two variables correspond to points of intersection of their graphs, because points of intersection satisfy both equations simultaneously.

8.EE.C.8b Solve systems of two linear equations in two variables algebraically, and estimate solutions by graphing the equations. Solve simple cases by inspection.

8.EE.C.8c Solve real-world and mathematical problems leading to two linear equations in two variables.

Also 8.F.A.3, A-CED.A.2, A-CED.A.3, A-CED.A.4, A-REI.B.3, A-REI.C.6, A-REI.D.10

1.1 Shirts and Caps
Solving Equations With Two Variables

The eighth-graders are selling T-shirts and caps to raise money for their end-of-year party. The profit from the fundraiser depends on the number of caps and the number of T-shirts sold.

End-of-Year Party!

PROFIT
- $5 profit per T-shirt
- $10 profit per cap

GOAL
- Raise $600

Problem 1.1

To plan for the fundraiser, class officers need to know how many T-shirts and caps to order and sell.

A Find the profit *P* if the students sell

1. 15 shirts and 10 caps.

2. 12 shirts and 20 caps.

3. 30 shirts and 50 caps.

4. *s* shirts and *c* caps.

Problem 1.1 *continued*

B **1.** Find five pairs of numbers for shirt and cap sales that will allow the students to make a profit of exactly $600.

2. Each answer from part (1) can be written as an ordered pair of numbers (s, c). The ordered pairs (s, c), which represent points on a graph, are *solutions* of the equation $5s + 10c = 600$. Plot the ordered pairs on a coordinate grid like the one below.

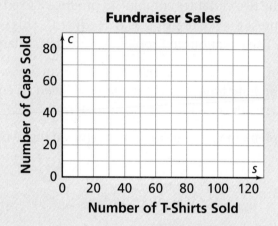

Fundraiser Sales

Number of Caps Sold (vertical axis: 0, 20, 40, 60, 80)

Number of T-Shirts Sold (horizontal axis: 0, 20, 40, 60, 80, 100, 120)

3. Use the graph to find three other ordered pairs that meet the profit goal.

4. Suppose the number of T-shirts sold was on the vertical axis and the number of caps sold was on the horizontal axis. Would the solutions change? Explain.

C For each equation

- find five solution pairs (x, y), including some with negative values.
- plot the solutions on a coordinate grid and draw the graph showing all possible solutions.

1. $x + y = 10$ **2.** $x - 2y = -4$

3. $-2x + y = 3$ **4.** $-3x + 2y = -4$

D Make a conjecture about the shape of the graph for any equation in the form $Ax + By = C$, where A, B, and C are fixed numbers. Explain why your conjecture is true.

A C E Homework starts on page 13.

1.2 Connecting $Ax + By = C$ and $y = mx + b$

There are two common forms of linear equations with two variables.

- When the values of one variable depend on those of another, it is common to express the relationship as $y = mx + b$. This equation is in **slope-intercept form.**

- When the values of the two variables combine to produce a fixed third quantity, you can express the relationship as $Ax + By = C$. This equation is in **standard form.** The equations in Problem 1.1 are in standard form.

The graph of each type of equation is a straight line. Since you know a lot about the graphs of **linear functions,** it is natural to ask: Given an equation in one form, can you rewrite the equation in the other form?

As you work on this Problem, look for connections between the two forms of linear equations.

Problem 1.2

A Four students tried to write $12x + 3y = 9$ in equivalent $y = mx + b$ form. Did each student get an equation equivalent to the original $Ax + By = C$ form? If so, explain the reasoning for each step. If not, tell what errors the student made.

Jared

$12x + 3y = 9$
$\qquad 3y = -12x + 9 \qquad (1)$
$\qquad y = -4x + 3 \qquad (2)$

Molly

$12x + 3y = 9$
$\qquad 3y = 9 - 12x \qquad (1)$
$\qquad y = 3 - 12x \qquad (2)$
$\qquad y = -12x + 3 \qquad (3)$

Mia

$12x + 3y = 9$
$\qquad 4x + y = 3 \qquad (1)$
$\qquad y = 3 - 4x \qquad (2)$
$\qquad y = -4x + 3 \qquad (3)$

Ali

$12x + 3y = 9$
$\qquad 3y = 9 - 12x \qquad (1)$
$\qquad y = 3 - 4x \qquad (2)$
$\qquad y = 4x - 3 \qquad (3)$

Problem 1.2 *continued*

B Write each equation in $y = mx + b$ form.

1. $x - y = 4$ **2.** $2x + y = 9$

3. $8x + 4y = -12$ **4.** $c = ax + dy$

C Write each equation in $Ax + By = C$ form.

1. $y = 5 - 3x$ **2.** $y = \frac{3}{4}x + \frac{1}{4}$

3. $x = 2y - 3$ **4.** $fy + 3 = gx - 15$

D Write a linear equation in slope-intercept form or standard form to represent each situation. Then, explain why your choice is the best representation.

1. Mary is selling popcorn for $5.00 per bucket and hotdogs for $4.75 each. After one hour, she makes $72.50.

2. Matt is in charge of selling roses for the Valentine's Day dance. The roses sell for $3.75 each. He estimates that the expenses for the roses are $25.00. Matt wants to write an equation for the profit.

3. Kaylee is mixing paint for an art project. She mixes 5 ounces of green paint with every 3 ounces of white paint. She needs 50 ounces of the paint mixture.

ACE Homework starts on page 13.

1.3 Booster Club Members
Intersecting Lines

At a school band concert, Christopher and Celine sell memberships for the band's booster club. An adult membership costs $10, and a student membership costs $5. At the end of the evening, the students had sold 50 memberships for a total of $400. The club president asked,

• How many of the new members are adults and how many are students?

You can answer the question by writing and solving equations that represent the question and the given information.

Problem 1.3

A Let *a* represent the number of $10 adult memberships and *s* represent the number of $5 student memberships.

1. What equation relates *a* and *s* to the $400 income total? Explain what each term of the equation represents.

2. Find three solutions for your equation from part (1).

3. What equation relates *a* and *s* to the total of 50 new members? Explain what each term of the equation represents.

4. Find three solutions for your equation from part (3).

5. Are there any pairs of values for *a* and *s* that satisfy both equations?

B 1. Graph the two equations from Question A on a grid like the one at the right. Does it matter which variable goes on which axis? Explain.

2. Determine the coordinates of the intersection point. Explain what the coordinates tell you about the numbers of adult and student memberships sold.

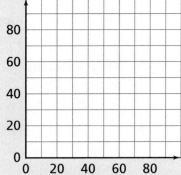

3. Could there be a common solution for the two equations that is *not* shown on your graph?

4. Describe situations you have studied in previous Units that are similar to this Problem.

The two equations you wrote to model the conditions of this Problem are called a **system of linear equations.** The coordinates of the intersection point satisfy both equations. These coordinates are the **solution of the system.**

C Use graphic or symbolic methods to solve each system of linear equations. Check your answer.

1. $x + y = 4$ and $x - y = -2$ 2. $2x + y = -1$ and $x - 2y = 7$

3. $-2x + y = 3$ and $-4x + 2y = 6$ 4. $-2x + y = 3$ and $-4x + 2y = 10$

A C E Homework starts on page 13.

Applications

1. For a fundraiser, students sell calendars and posters.

   a. What equation shows how the income *I* for the fundraiser depends on the number of calendars *c* and the number of posters *p* that are sold?

   b. What is the income if students sell 25 calendars and 18 posters?

   c. What is the income if students sell 12 calendars and 15 posters?

   d. What is the income if students sell 20 calendars and 12 posters?

   e. Find three combinations of calendar sales and poster sales that will give an income of exactly $100.

   f. Each answer in part (e) can be written as an ordered pair (*c*, *p*). Plot the ordered pairs on a coordinate grid.

   g. Use your graph to estimate three other (*c*, *p*) pairs that would meet the $100 goal.

2. Kateri saves her quarters and dimes. She plans to exchange the coins for paper money when the total value equals $10.

   a. How many coins does she need to make $10 if all the coins are quarters? If all the coins are dimes?

   b. What equation relates the number of quarters *x* and the number of dimes *y* to the goal of $10?

   c. Use the answers from part (a) to help you draw a graph showing all solutions to the equation.

   d. Use the graph to find five combinations of dimes and quarters that will allow Kateri to reach her goal.

3. Students in Eric's gym class must cover a distance of 1,600 meters by running or walking. Most students run part of the way and walk part of the way. Eric can run at an average speed of 200 meters per minute and walk at an average speed of 80 meters per minute.

   a. Suppose Eric runs for 4 minutes and walks for 8 minutes. How close is he to the 1,600-meter goal?

   b. Write an equation for the distance d Eric will cover if he runs for x minutes and walks for y minutes.

   c. Find three combinations of running and walking times for which Eric would cover 1,600 meters.

   d. Plot the ordered pairs from part (c) on a graph. Use the graph to estimate several other combinations of running and walking times for which Eric would cover 1,600 meters.

4. Kevin said that if you triple his age, the result will be 1 less than his mother's age.

   a. Which, if any, of these equations shows the relationship between Kevin's age x and his mother's age y? Choose all that are correct.

   $$3x - y = 1 \qquad y - 3x = 1 \qquad 3x + 1 = y \qquad 3x = 1 - y$$

   b. Find three pairs of values (x, y) that satisfy the equation relating Kevin's age and his mother's age. Plot these ordered pairs, and draw the line through the points.

   c. Use the graph to estimate three other ordered pairs that satisfy the equation. Use the equation to check the estimates.

Find three pairs of values (x, y) that satisfy each equation. Plot those points and use the pattern to find two more solution pairs. (Hint: What is y if $x = 0$? What is x if $y = 0$?)

5. $6 = 3x - 2y$

6. $10 = x + 2y$

7. $2x + y = 6$

8. $-3x + 4y = -4$

Write the equation in equivalent $Ax + By = C$ form. Then, identify the x-intercept, y-intercept, and slope.

9. $y = 4x - 2$

10. $y = -3x + 5$

11. $y = x - 7$

12. $y = 5x + 3$

13. $y = -8x - 12$

14. $y = -9x + 5$

For Exercises 15–20, write the equation in $y = mx + b$ form. Identify the x-intercept, y-intercept, and slope.

15. $-2x - y = -5$

16. $6x + 3y = -9$

17. $x - y = 4$

18. $3x + 4y = 12$

19. $-7x + 2y = -16$

20. $x - 5y = 55$

21. Look back over your work for Exercises 9–20. Look for patterns relating the standard form of the equation, $Ax + By = C$, to the x-intercept, y-intercept, and slope.

  a. Write a general formula for calculating the x-intercept from the values of A, B, and C.

  b. Write a general formula for calculating the y-intercept from the values of A, B, and C.

  c. Write a general formula for calculating the slope from the values of A, B, and C.

22. Tell which line below is the graph of each equation in parts (a)–(d). Explain.

  a. $2x + 3y = 9$

  b. $3x - 4y = 12$

  c. $x - 3y = 6$

  d. $3x + 2y = 6$

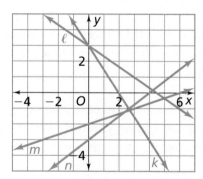

23. In Exercise 1, suppose the goal is to raise $600. One equation relating the calendar and poster sales to the $600 goal is $3c + 2p = 600$. Suppose the company donating the calendars and posters said they would provide a total of 250 items.

  a. What equation relates c and p to the 250 items donated?

  b. Graph both equations on the same grid. Find the coordinates of the intersection point. Explain what these coordinates tell you about the fundraising situation.

24. In Exercise 2, one equation relating Kateri's quarters and dimes to her goal of $10 (1,000 cents) is $25x + 10y = 1,000$. Suppose Kateri collects 70 coins to reach her goal.

   a. What equation relates x and y to the number of coins Kateri collected?

   b. Graph both equations on the same grid. Find the coordinates of the intersection point. Explain what these coordinates tell you about this situation.

25. In Exercise 3, one equation relating the times Eric spends running and walking to reach the goal of covering 1,600 meters is $200x + 80y = 1,600$. Suppose Eric runs and walks for a total of 12 minutes to reach his goal.

   a. What equation relates x and y to Eric's total time?

   b. Graph both equations on the same grid. Find the coordinates of the intersection point. Explain what these coordinates tell you about this situation.

26. In Exercise 4, one equation relating the ages of Kevin and his mother is $y - 3x = 1$. The sum of Kevin's age and his mother's age is 61 years.

   a. What equation relates Kevin's and his mother's ages to the total of their ages?

   b. Graph both equations on the same grid. Find the coordinates of the intersection point. Explain what these coordinates tell you about the ages of Kevin and his mother.

27. Use graphing methods to solve each system of equations. (**Hint:** If you are using a graphing calculator, you can determine a good graphing window by first finding the x- and y-intercepts of each graph.)

   a. $x - y = -4$ and $x + y = 6$

   b. $-2x + y = 3$ and $x + 2y = -9$

   c. $-2x + y = 1$ and $4x - 2y = 6$

Connections

For Exercises 28–33, solve the inequality. Then, write the solution using symbols, write the solution using words, and graph the solution on a number line.

28. $x + 3 < 5$

29. $x - 12 > -4$

30. $14 + x \leq -2$

31. $2x + 7 \geq -3$

32. $7x + 3 \leq -17 + 2x$

33. $-3 - 4x \geq 5x + 24$

34. The cost C to make T-shirts for a softball team is represented by the equation $C = 24 + 6N$, where N represents the number of T-shirts.

   a. Find the coordinates of a point that lies on the graph of this equation. Explain what the coordinates mean in this context.

   b. Find the coordinates of a point above the line. Explain what the coordinates mean in this context.

   c. Find the coordinates of a point below the line. Explain what the coordinates mean in this context.

35. a. Which of the following points lies on the line $y = 4x - 3$? Describe where the other three points are located in relation to the line.

       $(2, 1)$ $(2, 2)$ $(2, 5)$ $(2, 8)$

   b. Find another point that lies on the line $y = 4x - 3$. Find three more points that lie above the line.

   c. The points $(-2, -11)$ and $(3, 9)$ lie on the graph of $y = 4x - 3$. Use this information to find two points that make the inequality $y < 4x - 3$ true, and two points that make the inequality $y > 4x - 3$ true.

Write an equation of a line parallel to the given line.

36. $y = 4x + 6$

37. $-6x + y = 3$

38. $x + y = 9$

39. $x + 4y = -20$

40. $y = -\frac{3}{4}x - 2$

41. $7x + y = -12$

For Exercises 42–47, write an equation of a line perpendicular to the given line.

42. $y = -4x + 2$

43. $y = -\frac{2}{3}x - 7$

44. $y = 6x + 12$

45. $-2x + y = -1$

46. $x - 4y = 20$

47. $2x + 3y = 8$

48. Tell whether each ordered pair is a solution of $3x - 5y = 15$. Show how you know.

   a. $(-2, -4)$ **b.** $(0, -3)$ **c.** $(-10, 9)$

   d. $(-5, -6)$ **e.** $(-10, -9)$ **f.** $(-4, -5.4)$

49. The angle measures of the triangle are $x°$, $y°$, and $z°$.

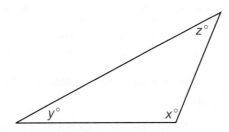

   a. What equation shows how z depends on x and y?

   b. Find five combinations of values for x and y for which the value of z is 40.

50. Multiple Choice Suppose k, m, and n are numbers and $k = m + n$. Which of the following statements must be true?

   A. $k - m = n$ **B.** $m - k = n$

   C. $2k = 2m + n$ **D.** $-n = k + m$

51. Multiple Choice Which equation is equivalent to $3x + 5y = 15$?

   F. $3x = 5y + 15$ **G.** $x = -5y + 5$

   H. $y = 0.6x + 3$ **J.** $y = -0.6x + 3$

52. Suppose you are given the linear equation $Ax + By = C$.

   a. What is the slope of every line parallel to this line?

   b. What is the slope of every line perpendicular to this line?

53. You will need two sheets of grid paper and two different cans with
paper labels (for example, clam chowder and stewed tomatoes cans).
On grid paper, trace the top and bottom of each can. Cut these out.
Now carefully remove the labels and trace these on grid paper.

  a. Estimate and compare the surface areas of the cans.
  (**Hint:** The surface area of a can = label + top + bottom or
  S.A. = $\ell w + 2\pi r^2$.)

  b. After Joel removes his two labels, he notices that the labels are the
  exact same size and shape. Explain how this can happen.

54. **Multiple Choice** Which values are solutions of the quadratic
equation $x^2 + 8x - 33 = 0$?

  A. $x = -11$ and $x = -3$

  B. $x = 11$ and $x = -3$

  C. $x = -11$ and $x = 3$

  D. $x = 11$ and $x = 3$

55. Use the graph of $y = x^2 + 8x - 33$ to find the solution of
each inequality.

  a. $x^2 + 8x - 33 > 0$ **b.** $x^2 + 8x - 33 < 0$

56. Tell whether each line has a slope of $-\frac{1}{2}$.

  a. $y = \frac{-1}{-2}x + 3$ **b.** $y = \frac{-1}{2}x + 3$

  c. $y = \frac{1}{-2}x + 3$ **d.** $y = -\frac{1}{2}x + 3$

57. a. What shape will this net make if it is cut out and folded?

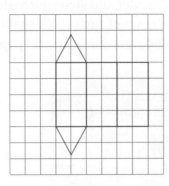

b. Find the surface area of the shape.

c. Find the volume of the shape.

Without graphing, decide whether the lines are *parallel*, *perpendicular*, or *neither*.

58. $3x + 6y = 12$ and $y = 10 + \frac{-1}{2}x$

59. $y = -x + 5$ and $y = x + 5$

60. $y = 2 - 5x$ and $y = -5x + 2$

61. $y = -3 + 5x$ and $y = \frac{-x}{5} + 3$

62. $10x + 5y = 20$ and $y = 10x + 20$

Extensions

63. Jasmine wants to run a marathon. She knows she will have to walk some of the 26.2 miles, but she wants to finish in 5 hours. She plans to run 10-minute miles and walk 15-minute miles. Let x represent the number of minutes Jasmine runs. Let y represent the number of minutes she walks.

  a. What equation relates x and y to the goal of completing the race in 5 hours?

  b. What equation relates x and y to the goal of covering 26.2 miles?

  c. For each equation, find several ordered-pair solutions (x, y). Then, plot the points with those coordinates and use the pattern to draw a graph of the equation. Graph both equations on the same grid.

  d. Use the graphs to estimate the combination of running and walking times that will allow Jasmine to complete the marathon in exactly 5 hours.

64. In Exercise 63, suppose Jasmine decides she wants to finish the marathon in less than 5 hours.

  a. Find five combinations of running and walking times that give a total time of less than 5 hours.

  b. Express the condition that the total running and walking times must be less than 5 hours as an inequality.

  c. Make a graph of all the solutions of the inequality.

  d. Graph the linear equation from Exercise 63, part (b) on the same grid as the inequality. Explain how the result shows Jasmine's options for running and walking times if she wants to finish the marathon in 5 hours or less.

Mathematical Reflections

1

In this Investigation, you used coordinate graphs to display solutions of linear equations in the form $Ax + By = C$ and to find solutions of systems of linear equations. The following questions will help you summarize what you have learned.

Think about these questions. Discuss your ideas with other students and your teacher. Then write a summary of your findings in your notebook.

1. **What** pattern will result from plotting all points (x, y) that satisfy an equation in the form $Ax + By = C$?

2. **How** can you change linear equations in the form $Ax + By = C$ to $y = mx + b$ form and vice versa? Explain when one form might be more useful than the other.

3. **How** can you use a graph to find values of x and y that satisfy systems of two linear equations in the form $Ax + By = C$?

Common Core Mathematical Practices

As you worked on the Problems in this Investigation, you used prior knowledge to make sense of them. You also applied Mathematical Practices to solve the Problems. Think back over your work, the ways you thought about the Problems, and how you used Mathematical Practices.

Ken described his thoughts in the following way:

In Problem 1.2, we wrote the equation $12x + 3y = 9$ as $y = 3 - 4x$ because we knew they were equivalent. We noticed that each form highlights a different part of the same equation.

If the value of one variable depended on another, the $y = mx + b$ form was more useful because the variable y was already isolated.

If the values of the two variables combined to produce a fixed value, the $Ax + Bx = C$ form was more useful because the constant was isolated.

Common Core Standards for Mathematical Practice

MP7 Look for and make use of structure.

- What other Mathematical Practices can you identify in Ken's reasoning?

- Describe a Mathematical Practice that you and your classmates used to solve a different Problem in this Investigation.

Solving Linear Systems Symbolically

Your work in Investigation 1 revealed key facts about solving linear equations.

- The solutions of equations in the form $Ax + By = C$ are ordered pairs of numbers.

- The graph of the solutions for an equation $Ax + By = C$ is a straight line.

- The solution of a system of two linear equations is the coordinates of the point where the lines intersect.

In *Say It With Symbols*, you solved systems of equations, such as the following:

> Ms. Lucero wants to install tiles around her square swimming pool. The equations below show the estimated costs C (in dollars) of buying and installing N border tiles.

$$\text{Cover and Surround It:} \quad C_C = 1,000 + 25(N - 12)$$

$$\text{Tile and Beyond:} \quad C_T = 740 + 32(N - 10)$$

For what number of tiles are the costs of the two companies equal?

Common Core State Standards

8.EE.C.8 Analyze and solve pairs of simultaneous linear equations.

8.EE.C.8a Understand that solutions to a system of two linear equations in two variables correspond to points of intersection of their graphs, because points of intersection satisfy both equations simultaneously.

8.EE.C.8c Solve real-world and mathematical problems leading to two linear equations in two variables.

Also **8.EE.C.8b, A-CED.A.2, A-CED.A.3, A-CED.A.4, A-REI.B.3, A-REI.C.5, A-REI.C.6, A-REI.D.10**

You can write the two equations as a system of two linear equations:

$$\begin{cases} C_C = 1{,}000 + 25(N - 12) \\ C_T = 740 + 32(N - 10) \end{cases}$$

You found solutions of this system in two ways by

- setting $C_C = C_T$ and solving for N. Then, you substituted N into one of the equations to find the cost.

- graphing the pair of equations. Then, you found the coordinates (C, N) of the intersection point of the two lines. The ordered pair is called the solution of the system. When you substitute the coordinates into each equation, the resulting statement is true.

Finding an exact solution is not always easy to do from a graph of the pair of linear equations. In this Investigation, you will develop symbolic methods for solving systems of linear equations.

2.1 Shirts and Caps Again
Solving Systems With $y = mx + b$

Recall the T-shirt and cap sale from Investigation 1.

- What two equations represent the relationship between the number of shirts sold and the number of caps sold?

- How can you find the number of shirts and the number of caps sold? Explain your reasoning.

Problem 2.1

A Check Nyla and Jimfa's solution strategies below.

Nyla

Write a system of two linear equations.

$$\begin{cases} c + s = 18 \\ 10c + 5s = 125 \end{cases}$$

Write equivalent equations.

$$\begin{cases} c = 18 - s \\ c = \dfrac{1}{10}(125 - 5s) \end{cases} \text{ or}$$

$$\begin{cases} c = 18 - s \\ c = 12.5 - 0.5s \end{cases}$$

Graph the two equations. The solution of the system is the point where the graphs of the equations meet.

Jimfa

Write a system of two linear equations.

$$\begin{cases} c + s = 18 \\ 10c + 5s = 125 \end{cases}$$

Write equivalent equations.

$$\begin{cases} c = -s + 18 \\ c = -0.5s + 12.5 \end{cases}$$

Write one linear equation.

$$-0.5s + 12.5 = -s + 18$$

Solve the linear equation for s. Then find the related value of c.

1. Do you agree with Nyla's reasoning? If not, explain why. If so, solve the system using her method.

2. Do you agree with Jimfa's reasoning? If not, explain why. If so, solve the system using his method.

3. How many shirts and caps did the class sell? Explain your reasoning.

B Use symbolic methods to find values of x and y that satisfy each system. Check your solution by substituting the values into the equations and showing that the resulting statements are true.

1. $\begin{cases} y = 1.5x - 0.4 \\ y = 0.3x + 5 \end{cases}$
2. $\begin{cases} x + y = 3 \\ x - y = -5 \end{cases}$
3. $\begin{cases} 3x - y = 30 \\ x + y = 14 \end{cases}$

4. $\begin{cases} x + 6y = 15 \\ -x + 4y = 5 \end{cases}$
5. $\begin{cases} x - y = -5 \\ -2x + 2y = 10 \end{cases}$
6. $\begin{cases} x - y = -5 \\ -2x + 2y = 8 \end{cases}$

Problem 2.1 *continued*

C Ming and Eun Mi discuss how to solve the system. $\begin{cases} x + y = 3 \\ x - y = -5 \end{cases}$

Ming says it would be easier to solve the system by writing each equation in the equivalent form $x = ny + c$. Eun Mi says it would be easier to solve the system by writing each equation in the equivalent form $y = mx + b$. Who is correct? Explain.

ACE Homework starts on page 32.

2.2 Taco Truck Lunch
Solving Systems by Combining Equations I

In Problem 2.1, you developed strategies for solving systems of equations by writing each equation in the equivalent form $y = mx + b$ or $x = ny + c$. Then you found the solution of the system by graphing or by solving one linear equation for x or y.

In this Problem, you will learn another strategy for solving linear systems.

Pablo and Jasmine each took their brothers out for lunch. They stopped at a taco truck where the prices were not posted.

After placing their orders, they compared what they bought with the total cost for each order.

Pablo and his brother got 6 tacos and 2 drinks for $9.

- Can you use this information to find the price of one taco? Of one drink? Explain.

Jasmine and her brother got 4 tacos and 2 drinks for $7.

- Does the additional information help you find the price of one taco? Of one drink? Explain.

> **?** What is the price of one taco and the price of one drink? Explain your reasoning.

Problem 2.2

A Pablo's younger brother Pedro used the orders and total prices to find the price of each taco and each drink.

When asked how he figured out the prices, Pedro said, "It's kind of like what we did in school with coins and pouches." Then he made the following sketch.

| T T T T T T + D D = $ $ $ $ $ $ $ $ $ |
| T T T T + D D = $ $ $ $ $ $ $ |

1. How does the sketch help you find the price of one taco and the price of one drink?

2. Find another way to use Pedro's sketch to solve the problem.

Problem 2.2 *continued*

B Pablo and Jasmine had just started studying systems of linear equations in algebra. They looked at Pedro's drawing and said, "We could write that as a system of equations."

1. Write an equation that represents the cost of Pablo's order and one that represents the cost of Jasmine's order. Use t for the price of each taco and d for the price of each drink.

2. What operations with the equations from part (1) match your way of using Pedro's sketch to find the prices t and d? Why do the operations make sense?

C In algebra class the next day, Pablo and Jasmine tried to solve the system of linear equations. $\begin{cases} x + 4y = 11 \\ x + y = 5 \end{cases}$

1. How could they represent the system with a sketch similar to the one Pedro drew of the taco truck orders?

2. How could the sketch and reasoning about the equations lead them to a solution of the system?

D Use diagrams or reasoning about equations to solve each system.

1. $\begin{cases} 3x + y = 4 \\ x + y = 5 \end{cases}$

2. $\begin{cases} 3x + 2y = 4 \\ x + 2y = 6 \end{cases}$

A C E Homework starts on page 32.

2.3 Solving Systems by Combining Equations II

Pablo and Jasmine showed their method for solving systems of linear equations. Their teacher then asked the class how they would solve the following system using the methods from Problem 2.2.

$$\begin{cases} 2x - y = 4 \\ x + y = 5 \end{cases}$$

Their classmate Samantha offered the following solution:

If $2x - y = 4$ and $x + y = 5$, then

$$(2x - y) + (x + y) = 4 + 5 \qquad (1)$$
$$3x = 9 \qquad (2)$$
$$x = 3 \qquad (3)$$
$$3 + y = 5 \qquad (4)$$
$$y = 2 \qquad (5)$$

- What reasoning justifies each step of her solution?

- Is her solution correct? Why or why not?

Pablo said, "Jasmine and I combined equations by subtracting equals from equals." Samantha said, "In my method, I combined equations by adding equals to equals." You will use both methods in this Problem.

Problem 2.3

A Use the methods of Pablo and Jasmine, and Samantha to solve each system.

1. $\begin{cases} -x + 4y = 2 \\ x + 2y = 5 \end{cases}$

2. $\begin{cases} 2x + 3y = 4 \\ 5x + 3y = -8 \end{cases}$

3. $\begin{cases} 2x - 3y = 4 \\ 5x - 3y = 7 \end{cases}$

4. $\begin{cases} 3x + 2y = 10 \\ 4x - y = 6 \end{cases}$

B In the T-shirt and cap sale, the equation $5s + 10c = 125$ related profit to the number of shirts and caps sold.

1. Find five solutions of the equation.

2. Samantha said, "If we had doubled the price of each item, we would have doubled the profit for the same numbers of shirts and caps sold." Do you agree with her reasoning? Why or why not?

3. Write Samantha's new equation. Check whether the solutions from part (1) are also solutions of the new equation.

C **1.** Is System B below equivalent to System A? Explain.

System A

$\begin{cases} 3x + 2y = 10 \\ 4x - y = 6 \end{cases}$

System B

$\begin{cases} 3x + 2y = 10 \\ 8x - 2y = 12 \end{cases}$

2. Use the combination method to solve System B.

3. Check that your solution also satisfies System A.

D For each system:

• Write an equivalent system that is easy to solve using the combination method.

• Solve the system.

• Check that your solution also satisfies the original system.

1. $\begin{cases} 2x + 2y = 5 \\ 3x - 6y = 12 \end{cases}$

2. $\begin{cases} x + 3y = 4 \\ 4x + 5y = 2 \end{cases}$

3. $\begin{cases} 2x + y = 5 \\ 3x - 2y = 15 \end{cases}$

4. $\begin{cases} -x + 2y = 5 \\ 5x - 10y = 11 \end{cases}$

A C E Homework starts on page 32.

Applications

1. A school is planning a Saturday Back-to-School Festival to raise funds for the school art and music programs. Some of the planned activities are a ring toss, frog jump, basketball free throws, and a golf putting green. The organizers are considering two pricing plans.

> Plan 1: $5 admission fee, $1 per game
>
> Plan 2: $2.50 admission fee, $1.50 per game

   a. Write equations that show how the cost y for playing the games at the festival depends on the number of games x that a participant chooses to play.

   b. Estimate the coordinates of the intersection point of the graphs of the two equations. Check to see if those coordinates are an exact solution of both equations.

   c. Use the expressions in the two cost equations to write and solve a single linear equation for the x-coordinate of the intersection point. Then use that x-value to find the y-coordinate of the intersection point.

   d. For what number of games would Plan 1 be a better deal for participants than Plan 2?

2. In Exercise 1, suppose the two pricing plans changed as follows. Complete parts (a)–(d) based on these two plans.

> Plan 1: $4.50 admission fee, $1 per game
>
> Plan 2: $3.50 admission fee, $1 per game

Solve each system of equations.

3. $\begin{cases} y = 6x + 4 \\ y = 4x - 2 \end{cases}$

4. $\begin{cases} y = 3x + 7 \\ y = 5x - 7 \end{cases}$

5. $\begin{cases} y = -2x - 9 \\ y = 12x + 19 \end{cases}$

6. $\begin{cases} y = -x + 16 \\ y = -x - 8 \end{cases}$

7. $\begin{cases} y = 17x - 6 \\ y = 12x + 44 \end{cases}$

8. $\begin{cases} y = -20x + 14 \\ y = -8x - 44 \end{cases}$

For Exercises 9–14, write the equation in $y = mx + b$ form.

9. $4x + 6y + 12 = 0$

10. $-7x + 9y + 4 = 0$

11. $-4x - 2y - 6 = 0$

12. $-x + 4y = 0$

13. $2x - 2y + 2 = 0$

14. $25x + 5y - 15 = 0$

15. A sixth-grade class sells pennants and flags. They earn $1 profit for each pennant sold and $6 profit for each flag sold. They sell 50 items in total for a profit of $115.

   a. Write two equations that represent the relationship between the number of pennants sold p and the number of flags sold f.

   b. How many pennants and how many flags were sold?

16. A seventh-grade class sells mouse pads and cell phone cases with their school logo on them. The class earns $2 profit for each mouse pad sold and $4 profit for each cell phone case sold. They sell 100 items in total for a profit of $268.

   a. Write two equations that represent the relationship between the number of mouse pads sold m and the number of cell phone cases sold c.

   b. How many mouse pads and how many cell phone cases were sold?

17. Write a system of equations that you can use to find the two numbers.

   a. Two numbers have a sum of 119 and a difference of 25.

   b. Two numbers have a sum of 71 and a difference of 37.

   c. Two numbers have a sum of 32 and a difference of 60.

   d. Two numbers have a sum of 180 and a difference of 45.

   e. If you know the sum and difference of two numbers, how can you use this information to find one of the two missing numbers? How do you find the second missing number?

18. On a hot summer day, Jay set up a lemonade stand. He kept track of how many glasses he sold on his phone.

a. Write two equations that relate the number of large glasses sold *l* and the number of small glasses sold *s*.

b. Solve the system of equations.

c. How many small glasses were sold?

d. How many large glasses were sold?

Pablo and Jasmine decide to try some other food trucks after eating at the taco truck in Problem 2.2. For Exercises 19–22, do the following.

a. Write two equations based on the information.

b. Solve the system of equations to determine the price of 1 serving of food and the price of 1 drink or bag of chips.

19. Pablo buys 3 servings of jambalaya and 2 drinks for $18.00. Jasmine buys 1 serving of jambalaya and 2 drinks for $9.00.

20. Pablo buys 4 sandwiches and 4 bags of chips for $24.00. Jasmine buys 8 sandwiches and 4 bags of chips for $43.00.

21. Pablo buys 3 loaves of zucchini bread and 5 cups of tea for $15.00. Jasmine buys 5 loaves of zucchini bread and 3 cups of tea for $21.00.

22. Pablo buys 6 apple pies and 2 juices for $39.00. Jasmine buys 2 apple pies and 4 juices for $18.00.

Solve each system by using the combination method.

23. $\begin{cases} 3x - 2y = 12 \\ -3x + 8y = -6 \end{cases}$

24. $\begin{cases} 4x + 9y = 7 \\ 4x - 9y = 9 \end{cases}$

25. $\begin{cases} 12x - 14y = -8 \\ -8x - 14y = 52 \end{cases}$

26. $\begin{cases} 5x + 15y = 10 \\ 5x - 10y = -40 \end{cases}$

27. $\begin{cases} -6x - 4y = 21 \\ -6x + 3y = 0 \end{cases}$

28. $\begin{cases} 2x - 3y = 14 \\ -x + 3y = -6 \end{cases}$

29. $\begin{cases} 3x + 2y = 17 \\ -2x - y = -12 \end{cases}$

30. $\begin{cases} 4x + 3y = 18 \\ 3x + 4y = 3 \end{cases}$

31. $\begin{cases} -2x + 6y = 42 \\ 4x - 3y = -12 \end{cases}$

32. Students in Mr. Coutley's class are playing the game "guess the date." For example, one student chooses a date (April 16), writes the date as an ordered pair (4, 16), and gives two clues.

Clue 1 "If I add the month number and the day number, the sum is 20."

Clue 2 "If I double the month number and add it to the day number, the sum is 24."

The other students try to determine the date based on the two clues. Find the date that each student is thinking of by writing and solving a system of two equations.

ANDREW

First Clue: If I double the month number and add it to double the day number, the sum is 26.

Second Clue: If I double the month number and then subtract double the day number, the difference is –18.

First Clue: If I double the month number and add the day number, the sum is 26.

Second Clue: If I multiply the month number by 10 and then subtract the day number, the difference is 10.

LARA

MARTHA

First Clue: The sum of triple the month number and double the day number is 62.

Second Clue: The difference of double the month number and the day number is 4.

First Clue: The sum of four times the month number and the day number is 42.

Second Clue: The sum of the month number and four times the day number is 33.

AHNA

Connections

For Exercises 33–38, solve the equation. Check the solution.

33. $3x + 12 = 24$

34. $-7x - 13 = 15$

35. $8 - 2x = 30$

36. $-7 + 9x = 38$

37. $-4 - 6x = -22$

38. $8x + 17 = -15$

39. For each part (a)-(f), find the value of y when $x = -2$.

    a. $y = 3x - 7$

    b. $3x - 2y = 10$

    c. $7x - 4y = 12$

    d. $x = 4y - 2$

    e. $3 = 2x - y$

    f. $12 = -3x - 4y$

Write an equation of the line satisfying the given conditions.

40. slope $= -4$, y-intercept $= 3$

41. slope $= \frac{2}{3}$, passes through the point $(3, 4)$

42. slope $= -3$, y-intercept $= 2$

43. passes through the points $(5, 4)$ and $(1, 7)$

For Exercises 44–49, identify the slope and y-intercept of the line.

44. $3x + 2y = 4$

45. $4x - 8y = 12$

46. $x - y = 7$

47. $y = 4x - 8$

48. $2y = 4x + 6$

49. $y = 9$

50. Two lines can intersect at 0 points (if they are parallel), 1 point, or an infinite number of points (if they are the same). In parts (a)-(d), give all the possible numbers of intersection points for the two figures. Make sketches to illustrate the possibilities.

    a. a circle and a straight line

    b. two circles

    c. a circle and a triangle

    d. a circle and a rectangle

51. A **chord** is a line segment joining two points on a **circle.** $\overline{AC}$ is a chord in the diagram at the right.

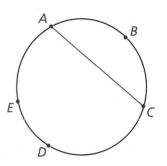

   a. How many chords can you draw by joining the labeled points on this circle?

   b. How many points inside the circle are intersection points of two or more of the chords from part (a)?

   c. The chords cut the circle into several nonoverlapping regions. How many regions are formed?

52. Multiple Choice Which point is *not* on the graph of $2x - 5y = 13$?

   A. $(9, 1)$ **B.** $(4, -1)$ **C.** $(0, 3.2)$ **D.** $(6.5, 0)$

53. The cylinder below represents an air conditioner with a radius of x feet and height of 2 feet.

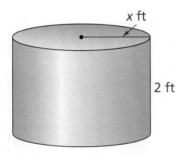

x ft

2 ft

   a. Draw a net of a cover for the air conditioner. The top and sides need to be covered, but not the bottom.

   b. Which equation below represents the area of the cover? Which represents the volume?

   $$y = 2\pi x^2 \qquad\qquad y = \pi x^2 + 4\pi x$$
   $$y = 2x^3 \qquad\qquad y = \pi x(x + 4)$$

54. Multiple Choice Kaya wants to fence off part of her yard for a garden. She has 150 feet of fencing. She wants a rectangular garden with a length 1.5 times its width. Which system represents these conditions?

   F. $\begin{cases} 1.5w = \ell \\ w + \ell = 150 \end{cases}$

   G. $\begin{cases} w = 1.5\ell \\ w + \ell = 150 \end{cases}$

   H. $\begin{cases} 2w = 3\ell \\ w + \ell = 75 \end{cases}$

   J. $\begin{cases} 3w = 2\ell \\ 2(w + \ell) = 150 \end{cases}$

55. Multiple Choice Which equation shows how to find one dimension of the garden described in Exercise 54?

A. $2.5w = 150$ **B.** $2.5\ell = 150$

C. $2w = 3(75 - w)$ **D.** $5w = 150$

For Exercises 56–59, write an equation that represents each line on the graph. Then, solve the system of equations symbolically.

56.

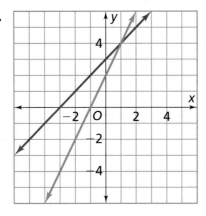

57.

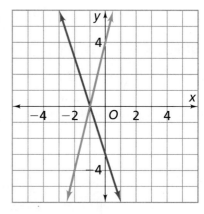

58.

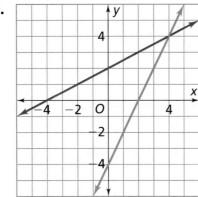

59.

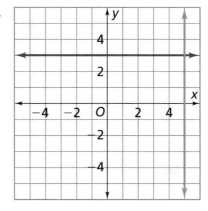

60. How does the solution of each system of equations in Exercises 56–59 relate to its the graph?

Write a system of equations that has each solution.

61. $x = 3$, $y = 2$ **62.** $x = 0$, $y = 0$

63. $x = -4$, $y = -2$ **64.** $x = \frac{1}{2}$, $y = \frac{1}{4}$

For Exercises 65–68, tell whether the table represents a linear, quadratic, exponential, or inverse variation relationship. Write an equation for the relationship.

65.

x	0	1	2	3	4	5	6	7
y	0	3	4	3	0	5	12	21

66.

x	−1	0	1	2	3	4	5	6
y	$\frac{1}{3}$	1	3	9	27	81	243	729

67.

x	1	3	4	6	9	10	12	18
y	2	8	11	17	26	29	35	53

68.

x	1	2	3	4	6	8	10	12
y	12	6	4	3	2	1.5	1.2	1

69. Use the tables of four linear equations.

Line a

x	−3	−2	−1	0
y	6	2	−2	−6

Line b

x	−3	−1	0	4
y	−6	−2	0	8

Line c

x	−3	1	0	3
y	6	2	3	0

Line d

x	4	6	8	10
y	5	6	7	8

What is the solution of the system of equations formed by

a. lines a and b?

b. lines a and c?

c. lines a and d?

d. lines b and c?

e. lines b and d?

f. lines c and d?

Solve each equation for x.

70. $5(x + 4) - 2x = 5 + 6x + 2x$

71. $2(x + 2) - 6x = 6x + 8 - 2x$

72. $x^2 - 7x + 12 = 0$

73. $x^2 + 5x - 6 = 0$

74. Match each equation with its corresponding graph below.

a. $y = 2^x - 1$ **b.** $y = -x^2 + 2x + 8$ **c.** $y = (x + 2)(x - 4)$

d. $y = 2^x$ **e.** $y = 2x^2$ **f.** $25 = x^2 + y^2$

Graph 1

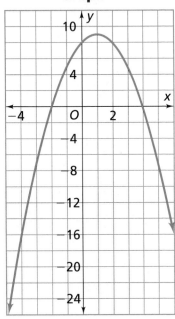

Graph 2

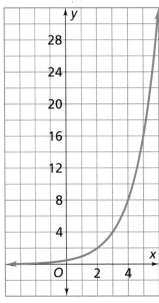

Graph 3

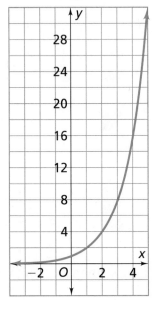

Graph 4

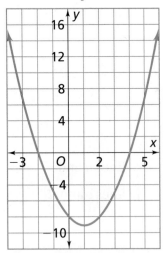

Graph 5

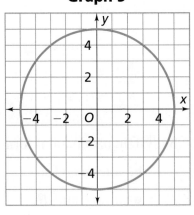

Graph 6

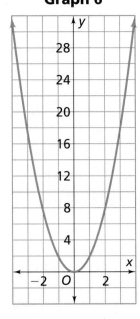

Extensions

75. Antonia and Marissa both babysit. Antonia charges $5.50 an hour. Marissa charges a base rate of $20.00, plus $.50 an hour.

   a. For each girl, write an equation showing how the charge depends on babysitting time.

   b. For what times are Marissa's charges less than Antonia's?

   c. Is there a time for which Antonia and Marissa charge the same amount?

76. Raj's age is 1 year less than twice Sarah's age. Toni's age is 2 years less than three times Sarah's age.

   a. Suppose Sarah's age is s years. What is Raj's age in terms of s?

   b. How old is Toni in terms of s?

   c. How old are Raj, Sarah, and Toni if the sum of their ages is 21?

77. Melissa and Trevor sell candy bars to raise money for a class field trip. Trevor sells 1 more than five times as many candy bars as Melissa sells. Together they sell 49 candy bars.

   a. Let m represent the number of candy bars Melissa sells. Let t represent the number of candy bars Trevor sells. Write a linear system to represent this situation.

   b. Solve your system to find the number of candy bars each student sells.

78. Solve each system by writing each equation in the equivalent form $y = mx + b$ or by using the combination method. You may get some interesting results. In each case, graph the equations and explain what the results indicate about the solution.

   a. $\begin{cases} x - 2y = 3 \\ -3x + 6y = -6 \end{cases}$
        b. $\begin{cases} x - y = 4 \\ -x + y = -4 \end{cases}$

   c. $\begin{cases} 2x - 3y = 4 \\ 4x - 6y = 7 \end{cases}$
        d. $\begin{cases} 4x - 6y = 4 \\ -6x + 9y = -6 \end{cases}$

79. The equation of the line is $y = \frac{4}{3}x$. The equation of the circle is $x^2 + y^2 = 25$.

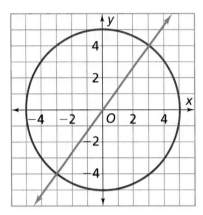

You can find the intersection points by solving the system below. Modify the combination method to solve the system.

$$\begin{cases} y = \frac{4}{3}x \\ x^2 + y^2 = 25 \end{cases}$$

80. In Investigation 1, you learned that the solution of a system of linear equations is the intersection point of their graphs. Determine the maximum number of intersection points for the graphs of each type of function given.

a. a quadratic function and a linear function

b. a quadratic function and a different quadratic function

c. a cubic function and a linear function

d. an inverse variation and a linear function

e. Which pairs of functions in parts (a)–(d) might not have an intersection?

81. Write a system in the form $\begin{cases} ax + by = c \\ dx + ey = f \end{cases}$ that has the given solution.

a. $(3, 7)$

b. $(-2, 3)$

c. no solution

82. Consider these equivalent systems.

$$\begin{cases} 2y - 3x = 0 \\ y + x = 75 \end{cases} \quad \text{and} \quad \begin{cases} 2y - 3x = 0 \\ 3y + 3x = 225 \end{cases}$$

a. Do the four equations in these two systems represent four different lines? Explain.

b. Adding the two equations in the second system gives $5y = 225$, or $y = 45$. Does $y = 45$ represent the same line as either equation in the system? Does its graph have anything in common with the lines in the system?

c. If you add the two equations in the first system, you get $3y - 2x = 75$. Does this equation represent the same line as either equation in the system? Does its graph have anything in common with the lines in the system?

d. What conjectures can you make about the results of adding any two linear equations? Consider the following questions:

- Will the result be a linear equation?

- Will the graph of the new equation have anything in common with the graphs of the original equations?

83. During math class, Mr. Krajewski gives Ben the following system.

$$\begin{cases} -3x - 6y + z = -7 \\ 6x + 3y - z = 6 \\ -9x - 3y + z = -7 \end{cases}$$

Ben thinks that he can solve the system if he adds the first equation to the second equation.

a. Why do you think Ben adds the two equations?

b. Is there another pair of equations Ben should add together?

c. Find the values of x, y, and z that satisfy the three equations.

84. A baking company makes two kinds of Sweeties, regular and double-stuffed.

Sweeties
1 serving = 3 cookies
160 Calories per serving

Double-Stuffed Sweeties
1 serving = 2 cookies
140 Calories per serving

a. How many wafers are in one serving of regular Sweeties? How many wafers are in one serving of double-stuffed Sweeties?

b. Let w represent the number of Calories in each wafer and f represent the number of Calories in each layer of filling.

   i. What equation shows the relationship between w, f, and the number of Calories in one serving of regular Sweeties?

   ii. What equation shows the relationship between w, f, and the number of Calories in one serving of double-stuffed Sweeties?

c. Solve the system of equations from part (b) to find the number of Calories in each Sweetie wafer and each layer of filling.

Mathematical Reflections

In this Investigation, you learned several strategies for finding solutions of systems of linear equations. The following questions will help you summarize what you have learned.

Think about these questions. Discuss your ideas with other students and your teacher. Then write a summary of your findings in your notebook.

1. **What** is the goal in solving a system of linear equations?

2. **What** strategies can you use to solve a system of linear equations?

3. **How** can you check a possible solution of a system of linear equations?

Common Core Mathematical Practices

As you worked on the Problems in this Investigation, you used prior knowledge to make sense of them. You also applied Mathematical Practices to solve the Problems. Think back over your work, the ways you thought about the Problems, and how you used Mathematical Practices.

Tori described her thoughts in the following way:

When we were solving systems of equations in Problem 2.1, some of us graphed the equations and some of us used symbolic methods. We were surprised that both of these methods gave the same results.

Both methods showed that the system in Question B, part (6) had no solution. The lines were parallel. The system in Question B, part (5) produced the same line, which means that the system had an infinite number of solutions. Then we remembered that we studied similar situations in *Moving Straight Ahead* for linear equations.

Common Core Standards for Mathematical Practice

MP8 Look for and express regularity in repeated reasoning.

- What other Mathematical Practices can you identify in Tori's reasoning?

- Describe a Mathematical Practice that you and your classmates used to solve a different Problem in this Investigation.

Investigation 3

Systems of Functions and Inequalities

Many businesses have contracts with private companies to provide security alarms and to respond to break-ins. Suppose the owners of a shopping center get bids from two reliable security companies.

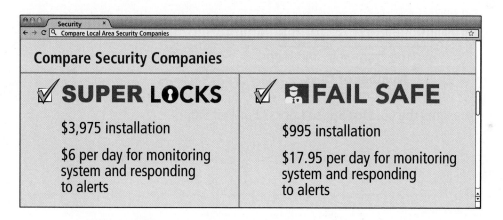

Compare Security Companies

✓ SUPER LOCKS

$3,975 installation

$6 per day for monitoring system and responding to alerts

✓ FAIL SAFE

$995 installation

$17.95 per day for monitoring system and responding to alerts

- How could you use linear functions to compare the costs for the two security companies?

- What patterns do you expect to see in the graphs of these functions?

- How can you use a graph to answer questions about which company offers the best price?

Common Core State Standards

8.EE.C.8a Understand that solutions to a system of two linear equations in two variables correspond to points of intersection of their graphs, because points of intersection satisfy both equations simultaneously.

8.EE.C.8c Solve real-world and mathematical problems leading to two linear equations in two variables.

Also A-CED.A.1, A-CED.A.2, A-CED.A.3, A-REI.B.3, A-REI.B.4, A-REI.B.4b, A-REI.C.7, A-REI.D.10, A-REI.D.12

3.1 Comparing Security Services
Linear Inequalities

The cost of security services from Super Locks and Fail Safe depends on the number of days that the company provides service. The graph below shows the bids for both companies.

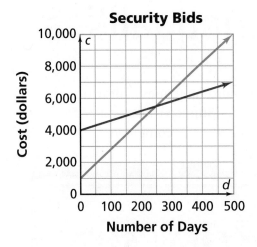

Security Bids

- Which line represents the cost for Super Locks? For Fail Safe?

Problem 3.1

A   Use the graph above to estimate the answers to these questions. Explain your reasoning in each case.

    1. For what number of days will the costs for the two companies be the same? What is that cost?

    2. For what numbers of days will Super Locks cost less than Fail Safe?

    3. For what numbers of days will Fail Safe cost less than Super Locks?

B   **1.** For each company, write an equation for the cost c for d days of security services.

    2. For Question A, parts (1)–(3), write an equation or inequality that you can use to answer each question.

Problem **3.1** *continued*

C Solve each equation or inequality by graphing a pair of linear functions.

1. $2x + 1 = 0.5x + 4$ **2.** $2x + 1 < 0.5x + 4$ **3.** $2x + 1 > 0.5x + 4$

4. $x - 2 = 6 - x$ **5.** $x - 2 > 6 - x$ **6.** $x - 2 < 6 - x$

7. $3x + 4 = 13$ **8.** $3x + 4 \leq 13$ **9.** $3x + 4 \geq 13$

D Francis recalls that he used number-line graphs to show solutions of inequalities in *Moving Straight Ahead*. For Question C, part (8) he graphed the solutions of the inequality $3x + 4 \leq 13$ on a number line, as shown below. The solutions are $x \leq 3$.

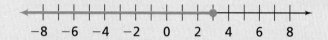

He used the number-line graph shown below to represent the solutions of the inequality $3x + 4 < 13$. The solutions are $x < 3$.

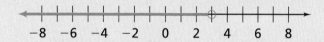

1. How do the solutions of $3x + 4 \leq 13$ on a coordinate grid relate to the solutions on a number line?

2. Draw number-line graphs to represent solutions of each inequality.

a. $2x + 1 < 0.5x + 4$

b. $2x + 1 > 0.5x + 4$

c. $2x + 1 \geq 0.5x + 4$

A C E Homework starts on page 54.

3.2 Solving Linear Inequalities Symbolically

Graphing methods are helpful for estimating solutions of inequalities. If you want exact results, you can use symbolic reasoning.

You already know how to use properties of equality to solve linear equations. To solve **linear inequalities**, you will learn to use the properties of operations on inequalities.

Problem 3.2

Ⓐ Suppose that two numbers q and r are related by the inequality $q < r$. Draw a number line such as the one below.

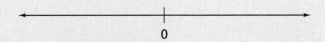

0

Locate points to represent the numbers q and r when

1. both q and r are positive numbers.

2. both q and r are negative numbers.

3. one number is negative and the other is positive.

Ⓑ Suppose $q < r$.

- Complete each statement below with an inequality symbol ($<$ or $>$) so that the result is true for all values of q and r.

- Use the number-line graphs from Question A and ideas about geometric transformations to explain each answer.

- If it is not possible to write an inequality statement that is true for all values of q and r, give examples to show why that is the case.

1. $q + 23 \; \blacksquare \; r + 23$ **2.** $q - 35 \; \blacksquare \; r - 23$ **3.** $14q \; \blacksquare \; 14r$

4. $-6q \; \blacksquare \; -6r$ **5.** $\frac{q}{5} \; \blacksquare \; \frac{r}{5}$ **6.** $\frac{q}{-3} \; \blacksquare \; \frac{r}{-3}$

Ⓒ What do your results from Question B suggest about how working with inequalities is similar to and different from working with equations?

Problem **3.2** *continued*

D Use symbolic reasoning to solve each inequality. Then, make a number-line graph to show the solutions.

1. $3x + 17 < 47$

2. $43 < 8x - 9$

3. $-6x + 9 < 25$

4. $14x - 23 < 5x + 13$

5. $18 < -4x + 2$

6. $3{,}975 + 6x < 995 + 17.95x$

A)C)E Homework starts on page 54.

3.3 Operating at a Profit
Systems of Lines and Curves

In the last Problem, you found that working with linear inequalities was similar to working with linear equations when operations involved positive numbers. When operations involved negative numbers, some differences occurred. Hector summarizes the results below:

If $p < q$ and a is positive, then
$$p + a < q + a$$
$$p - a < q - a$$
$$ap < aq$$

If $p < q$ and b is negative, then
$$p + b < q + b$$
$$p - b < q - b$$
$$bp > bq$$

In *Variables and Patterns* and *Say It With Symbols*, you studied the business plans of students who operate bicycle tours. The income and operating costs of the business both depend on the number of customers n.

Income	Operating Cost
$I = 400n - 10n^2$	$C = 150n + 1{,}000$

You found ways to find the break-even point, which is when income equals operating cost. You can also find the break-even point by thinking about these two equations as a system of functions.

- When would the tour business make a profit?

- When would it lose money?

- When would it simply break even?

- How can you use symbolic reasoning to solve this system of equations to answer these questions?

As with linear systems, it helps to begin with graphs that model the business conditions. Then, you can use symbolic reasoning to find the exact values of the coordinates of the points that answer your questions.

Problem 3.3

 A 1. Graph the income and cost functions on the same coordinate grid with the number of customers n on the horizontal axis.

2. Write an equation or inequality relating the two functions that you could use to answer each question.

    a. For what numbers of customers will income equal operating costs?

    b. For what numbers of customers will operating costs exceed income?

    c. For what numbers of customers will income exceed operating costs?

3. **a.** Use your graphs from part (1) to estimate solutions of the equations and inequalities you wrote in part (2). Explain how you know that your estimates are reasonably accurate.

    b. Describe how you could find exact solutions of the equations and inequalities from part (2).

Problem 3.3 *continued*

B Use ideas from your work in Question A to solve the following equations and inequalities.

  1. $x^2 - 4x + 4 = 2x - 1$

  2. $x^2 - 4x + 4 < 2x - 1$

  3. $x^2 - 4x + 4 > 2x - 1$

  4. $-x^2 + 4x + 2 = x - 2$

  5. $-x^2 + 4x + 2 < x - 2$

  6. $-x^2 + 4x + 2 > x - 2$

C In *Looking for Pythagoras*, you learned that the points on the graph of a circle with radius r and center $(0, 0)$ are solutions of the equation $x^2 + y^2 = r^2$. Use this fact to estimate the solutions of the systems of equations shown in the graph below.

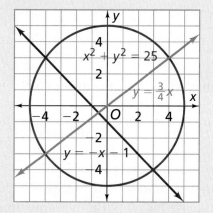

  1. $\begin{cases} x^2 + y^2 = 25 \\ y = \frac{3}{4}x \end{cases}$ **2.** $\begin{cases} x^2 + y^2 = 25 \\ y = -x - 1 \end{cases}$

  3. Describe how you could find exact solutions of the systems in parts (1) and (2).

A C E Homework starts on page 54.

Applications

1. Sam needs to rent a car for a one-week trip in Oregon. He is considering two companies.

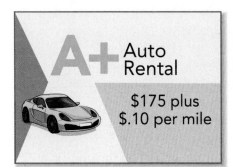

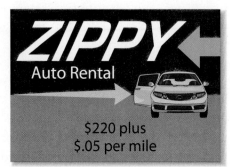

a. Write an equation relating the rental cost for each company to the number of miles driven.

b. Graph the equations.

c. Under what circumstances is the rental cost the same for both companies? What is that cost?

d. Under what circumstances is renting from Zippy cheaper than renting from A+?

e. Suppose Sam rents a car from A+ and drives 225 miles. What is his rental cost?

2. Mariana lives 1,250 meters from school. Ming lives 800 meters from school. Both students leave for school at the same time. Mariana walks at an average speed of 70 meters per minute, while Ming walks at an average speed of 40 meters per minute. Mariana's route takes her past Ming's house.

a. Write equations that show Mariana and Ming's distances from school t minutes after they leave their homes.

Answer parts (b)–(d) by writing and solving equations or inequalities.

b. When, if ever, will Mariana catch up with Ming?

c. How long will Mariana remain behind Ming?

d. At what times is the distance between the two students less than 20 meters?

3. Suppose s and t are two numbers and that $s > t$. Determine whether each inequality must be true.

    a. $s + 15 > t + 15$ **b.** $s - (-22) > t - (-22)$

    c. $s \times 0 > t \times 0$ **d.** $\frac{s}{-6} > \frac{t}{-6}$

    e. $\frac{s}{6} > \frac{t}{6}$ **f.** $s(-3) < t(-4)$

For Exercises 4–7, solve the inequality. Then, graph the solution on a number line.

4. $12 < 7x - 2$ **5.** $2x + 12 > 32$

6. $4x - 17 \leq 31$ **7.** $-16x - 12 > 14 - 10x$

8. Use the graph below to estimate solutions for the inequalities and equations in parts (a)–(f). Then, use symbolic reasoning to check your estimates.

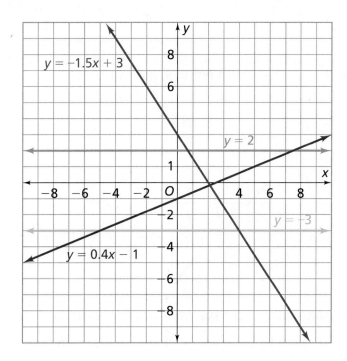

    a. $0.4x - 1 > 2$ **b.** $0.4x - 1 > -3$

    c. $-1.5x + 3 > 2$ **d.** $-1.5x + 3 < -3$

    e. $-1.5x + 3 = 0.4x - 1$ **f.** $-1.5x + 3 > 0.4x - 1$

9. When a soccer ball is kicked into the air, its height h in feet at any time t seconds later can be estimated by the function $h = -16t^2 + 32t$. For each question, write and solve an equation or inequality.

   a. When does the ball return to the ground ($h = 0$ feet)?

   b. When is the ball 12 feet above the ground?

   c. When is the ball at least 12 feet above the ground?

   d. When is the ball at most 12 feet above the ground?

   e. When is the ball 16 feet above the ground?

10. Solve each equation or inequality. Sketch the graphs of the functions that are associated with each equation or inequality. Explain how to find the solutions using the graphs.

   a. $-x^2 + 4x - 4 = -2x + 4$ b. $-x^2 + 4x - 4 < -2x + 4$

   c. $-x^2 + 4x - 4 > -2x + 4$ d. $x^2 - 5x = 6$

   e. $x^2 - 5x < 6$ f. $x^2 - 5x > 6$

11. The graph below shows a circle with radius 4 and two lines intersecting the circle.

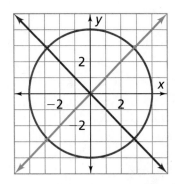

   - Estimate the solution(s) of the systems of equations using the graph.
   - Check your estimates by substituting them into the equations.
   - Find exact solution(s) of each system.

   a. $\begin{cases} x^2 + y^2 = 16 \\ y = x \end{cases}$ b. $\begin{cases} x^2 + y^2 = 16 \\ y = -x \end{cases}$

Connections

Calculate the *y*-value for the given *x*-value.

12. $y = 3x + 2$ when $x = -2$

13. $y = -3x + 4$ when $x = 9$

14. $y = \frac{1}{2}x - 4$ when $x = 24$

15. $y = -5x - 7$ when $x = \frac{1}{5}$

16. $y = \frac{2}{3}x - 12$ when $x = -18$

17. $y = -\frac{1}{4}x - \frac{3}{4}$ when $x = -6$

Graph the system of equations and estimate the point of intersection.
Then, use symbolic reasoning to check whether your estimate
is accurate.

18. $y = 2x + 4$ and $y = \frac{1}{2}x - 2$

19. $y = x + 5$ and $y = -3x + 3$

20. $y = 3$ and $y = 6x - 3$

21. $x = 2$ and $y = -\frac{2}{5}x + 4$

Write an equation for the line satisfying the given conditions.

22. slope $= 2$, *y*-intercept $= -3$

23. slope $= -4$, passes through $(0, 1.5)$

24. passes through $(-2, 1)$ and $(4, -3)$

25. passes through $(4, 0)$ and $(0, 3)$

Identify the slope, *x*-intercept, and *y*-intercept of the line.

26. $y = 7x - 3$

27. $y = -3x + 4$

28. $y = \frac{2}{3}x + 12$

29. $y = -\frac{1}{4}x - 5$

30. $y = \frac{3}{4} - 17x$

31. $y = -\frac{2}{3}(x + 10)$

**For Exercises 32–37, copy each pair of expressions. Insert <, >, or =
to make a true statement.**

32. $-18 \div (-3)$ ■ $-24 \div (-4)$ **33.** $1{,}750(-12)$ ■ $1{,}749(-12)$

34. $5(18 - 24)$ ■ $90 - (-120)$ **35.** $-8(-5)$ ■ $-7(-5)$

36. $4[-3 - (-7)]$ ■ $4(-3) - 4(-7)$ **37.** $-5(-4)^2$ ■ $-4(-5)^2$

38. Write an equation or inequality that tells whether each point is
inside, outside, or on the circle with a radius of 10 and centered
at $(0, 0)$.

     a. $(6, 8)$ **b.** $(7, 7)$ **c.** $(-7, -7)$

     d. $(-6, 8)$ **e.** $(-7, 8)$ **f.** $(-7, -8)$

**For Exercises 39–44, copy each pair of fractions. Insert <, >, or = to
make a true statement.**

39. $\frac{6}{8}$ ■ $\frac{-18}{24}$ **40.** $\frac{6}{8}$ ■ $\frac{7}{9}$ **41.** $\frac{6}{8}$ ■ $\frac{-7}{9}$

42. $\frac{6}{8}$ ■ $\frac{-18}{-24}$ **43.** $\frac{6}{8}$ ■ $\frac{-7}{-9}$ **44.** $\frac{8}{6}$ ■ $\frac{-9}{7}$

45. Use the figures below for parts (a)-(f). Insert <, >, or = to make
true statements.

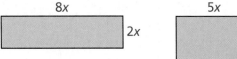
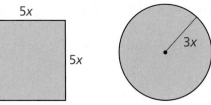

     a. perimeter of square ■ perimeter of rectangle

     b. area of square ■ area of rectangle

     c. perimeter of square ■ circumference of circle

     d. area of square ■ area of circle

     e. perimeter of rectangle ■ circumference of circle

     f. area of rectangle ■ area of circle

46. The gender of a newborn child is nearly equally likely to be a boy or a girl. Consider the patterns likely to occur in a family with three children.

Note: In the following statements, $P(Q)$ is used to indicate the probability that event Q occurs.

Copy parts (a)–(d). Insert $<$, $=$, or $>$ to make true statements.

a. $P(\text{all boys})$ ■ $P(\text{all girls})$

b. $P(\text{exactly one boy})$ ■ $P(\text{exactly 2 girls})$

c. $P(\text{BGB})$ ■ $P(\text{BBG})$

d. $P(\text{two boys and one girl})$ ■ $P(\text{all girls})$

47. Multiple Choice If $w = 3x + c$, what is the value of x?

A. 3

B. $\frac{w - c}{3}$

C. $w - c$

D. $\frac{w + c}{3}$

48. Suppose $\frac{a}{b}$ and $\frac{c}{d}$ are two nonzero fractions and $\frac{a}{b} < \frac{c}{d}$.

a. Give an example of values of a, b, c, and d that satisfy $\frac{a}{b} < \frac{c}{d}$ and also $\frac{b}{a} < \frac{d}{c}$.

b. Give an example of values of a, b, c, and d that satisfy $\frac{a}{b} < \frac{c}{d}$ and also $\frac{b}{a} > \frac{d}{c}$.

49. Multiple Choice Which function's graph is perpendicular to the graph of $y = 2.5x + 4$?

A. $y = 2.5x$

B. $y = 0.4x$

C. $y = -0.4x$

D. $y = -2.5x$

50. Use a table or graph of $y = 5(2^x)$ to estimate the solution of the inequality $5(2^x) > 1{,}000$.

For Exercises 51–56, write the expression for x in factored form. Then, find the x- and y-intercepts for the graph of the function.

51. $y = x^2 + 4x$

52. $y = x^2 + 4x + 4$

53. $y = x^2 + 3x - 10$

54. $y = x^2 - 8x + 16$

55. $y = x^2 - 4$

56. $y = x^2 + 4x + 3$

57. Multiple Choice Which expression is the factored form of $x + 2x + 6$?

F. $3x + 6$ **G.** $2(x + 3)$ **H.** $3(x + 2)$ **J.** $3(x + 6)$

Extensions

58. In parts (a)–(d), find values of x that satisfy the given conditions. Then, graph the solution on a number line.

     a. $x + 7 < 4 \; or \; x + 3 > 9$
     (**Hint:** Find the x-values that satisfy one inequality or the other, or both.)

     b. $3x + 4 < 13 \; and \; 12 < 6x$
     (**Hint:** Find the x-values that satisfy both inequalities.)

     c. $5x - 6 > 2x + 18 \; or \; -3x + 5 > 8x - 39$

     d. $-11x - 7 < -7x + 33 \; and \; 9 + 2x > 11x$

59. Suppose m and n are positive whole numbers and $m < n$. Tell whether each statement is always true.

     a. $2^m < 2^n$ **b.** $m^2 < n^2$ **c.** $0.5^m < 0.5^n$ **d.** $\frac{1}{m} < \frac{1}{n}$

60. Solve these quadratic inequalities.
(**Hint:** Use a graph or table of $y = 5x^2 + 7$ to estimate the solutions. Then adapt the reasoning used to solve linear inequalities to check the accuracy of your estimates.)

     a. $5x^2 + 7 \leq 87$ **b.** $5x^2 + 7 > 87$

61. Solve these exponential inequalities.
(**Hint:** Use a graph or table of $y = 2(3^x) - 8$ to estimate the solutions. Then adapt the reasoning used to solve linear inequalities to check the accuracy of your estimates.)

     a. $2(3^x) - 8 < 46$ **b.** $2(3^x) - 8 > 10$

Mathematical Reflections

In this Investigation, you learned graphic and symbolic methods for solving systems of linear equations and linear inequalities. The following questions will help you summarize what you have learned.

Think about these questions. Discuss your ideas with other students and your teacher. Then write a summary of your findings in your notebook.

1. **How** can you use coordinate graphs to solve linear equations such as $ax + b = cx + d$ and linear inequalities such as $ax + b < cx + d$?

2. **How** can you use symbolic reasoning to solve inequalities such as $ax + b < cx + d$?

3. **What** strategies can you use to solve systems of equations and inequalities that involve linear and quadratic functions or lines and circles?

Common Core Mathematical Practices

As you worked on the Problems in this Investigation, you used prior knowledge to make sense of them. You also applied Mathematical Practices to solve the Problems. Think back over your work, the ways you thought about the Problems, and how you used Mathematical Practices.

Sophie described her thoughts in the following way:

Our group had a discussion about which representation we thought was most useful for finding solutions of a system with one linear and one quadratic function. We used both graphical and symbolic methods.

Several of us thought that the graphs provided a powerful visual picture of what the symbols represented. This was similar to systems of linear equations. The graphs illustrated why sometimes there are only two solutions, one solution, or no solution.

Common Core Standards for Mathematical Practice
MP5 Use appropriate tools strategically.

- What other Mathematical Practices can you identify in Sophie's reasoning?

- Describe a Mathematical Practice that you and your classmates used to solve a different Problem in this Investigation.

4

Systems of Linear Inequalities

Investigation 3 focused on strategies for solving inequalities with one variable such as $3x + 4 < 13$ and $14x - 23 < 5x + 13$. Many problems, however, involve two or more variables.

In earlier Investigations, you applied your knowledge of simple linear equations to solve equations or systems of equations with two variables. You can also apply what you have learned about simple inequalities to solve inequalities or systems of inequalities with two variables in the form $Ax + By < C$.

4.1 Limiting Driving Miles
Inequalities With Two Variables

Automobiles are a major source of air pollution. When Jarod studied the effects of this pollution on global climate change, he decided to take a look at his family's driving habits. His family has two vehicles, a car and an SUV. His parents estimate that the family drives about 1,200 miles each month. They decide to try to limit their driving to no more than 1,000 miles each month.

• What are the variables in the situation? How are they related?

Common Core State Standards

8.EE.C.8b Solve systems of two linear equations in two variables algebraically, and estimate solutions by graphing the equations. Solve simple cases by inspection.

8.EE.C.8c Solve real-world and mathematical problems leading to two linear equations in two variables.

A-CED.A.3 Represent constraints by equations or inequalities, and by systems of equations and/or inequalities, and interpret solutions as viable or non-viable options in a modeling context.

Also A-CED.A.2, A-REI.C.6, A-REI.D.10, A-REI.D.12

Problem 4.1

A

1. Find ten possible pairs (*car miles, SUV miles*) that give a total of no more than 1,000 miles.

2. On a copy of the grid below, plot the ten points you found in part (1).

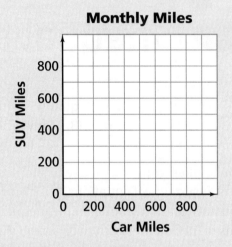

3. Are there other possible pairs (*car miles, SUV miles*) that give a total of no more than 1,000 miles? Explain.

4. A *region* is a part of a graph or plane. Describe the region where points representing totals of no more than 1,000 miles are located.

5. In what region are the points that meet the goal of less than 1,000 miles per month? How does this region compare to the region in part (4)?

B Suppose Jarod's family wants to limit their driving to no more than 800 miles per month.

1. Draw a graph of pairs (*car miles, SUV miles*) that meet this condition.

2. Describe the region of the graph that includes all the points that represent driving no more than 800 miles.

Problem 4.1 continued

C Let c represent the number of miles driven using the car. Let s represent the number of miles driven using the SUV. Write inequalities to model the following situations.

1. a total of no more than 1,000 miles driven using both vehicles

2. a total of no more than 800 miles driven using both vehicles

3. How are the inequalities you wrote in parts (1) and (2) related to your work in Questions A and B?

A C E Homework starts on page 72.

4.2 What Makes a Car Green?
Solving Inequalities by Graphing I

Carbon dioxide (CO_2) is a major factor in global climate change. Jarod finds out the amount of CO_2 that his family's vehicles emit.

This SUV emits 1.25 pounds of carbon dioxide per mile.

This car emits 0.75 pounds of carbon dioxide per mile.

? • Suppose Jarod's family wants to limit CO_2 emissions from their car and SUV to *at most* 600 pounds per month. What inequality would model this condition?

• What would a graph of the solutions for this inequality look like?

Problem 4.2

Ⓐ Suppose Jarod's family wants their total CO_2 emissions to be *exactly* 600 pounds per month.

   1. Give six examples of pairs (*car miles, SUV miles*) that meet this condition.

   2. Write an equation to model this condition.

   3. Graph your equation.

Ⓑ Suppose the family wants to limit their total CO_2 emissions to at most 600 pounds per month.

   1. Write an inequality that describes the possibilities for the number of miles they can drive that meet this condition.

   2. What is one solution (*car miles, SUV miles*) that meets this condition?

   3. Draw a graph displaying the solutions of your inequality from part (1). Describe the regions.

Ⓒ Soo's family has a minivan and a hybrid car. The minivan emits 1.2 pounds of CO_2 per mile. The hybrid car emits 0.5 pounds of CO_2 per mile. The family wants to limit their total emissions to at most 500 pounds per month.

   1. The family plans to drive both vehicles. Write an inequality to describe the possibilities for the number of miles they can drive each vehicle.

   2. Draw a graph displaying the pairs (*minivan miles, hybrid miles*) that satisfy the inequality you wrote in part (1).

ⒶⒸⒺ Homework starts on page 72.

4.3 Feasible Points
Solving Inequalities by Graphing II

In Problem 4.2, you graphed ordered pairs of driving mileage that would limit CO_2 emissions by Jarod and Soo's families. You discovered that the solutions of the inequalities are triangular regions. You also had to consider the fact that mileage and emission data cannot be negative numbers. In other words, all **feasible points** are in the first quadrant.

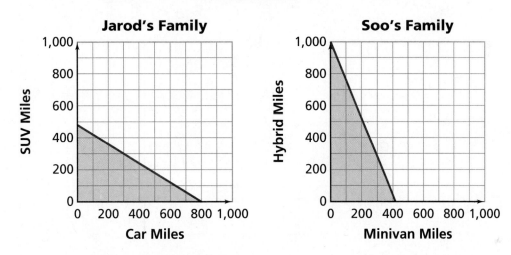

Some inequalities have solutions that are not limited to positive numbers. For example, one solution for $3x + 5y > 15$ is $(-1, 5)$. The region of feasible points for such inequalities will be different from those for the CO_2 emission problems.

Use what you have learned about graphs of linear inequalities to explore the possible shapes of feasible regions.

Problem 4.3

A Match each inequality with its graph, if possible. The solutions are shown by the shaded region. Be prepared to explain your strategies for matching the inequalities and graphs.

1. $y - 3x \geq 6$ **2.** $x - 3y \geq 6$ **3.** $3x + y \leq 6$

4. $x + 3y \leq 6$ **5.** $x - 3y \leq 6$ **6.** $y \geq -3x$

7. $y \leq -3x$ **8.** $x \geq -3$ **9.** $y \geq -3$

a.

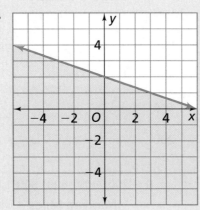

b.

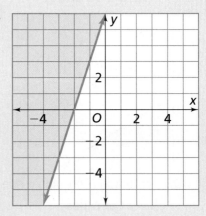

c.

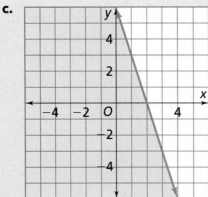

d.

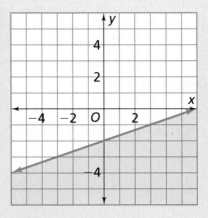

Problem **4.3** *continued*

e.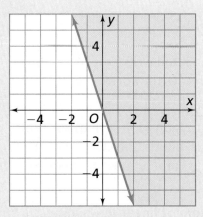

f.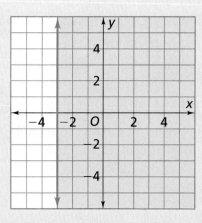

g.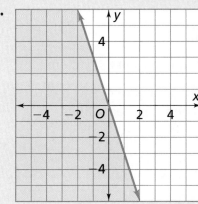

h.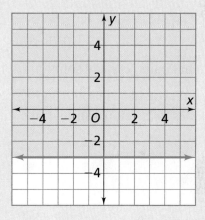

B Refer to the inequalities in parts (1)–(4) of Question A.

　1. Rewrite each inequality in either $y \leq mx + b$ or $y \geq mx + b$ form.

　2. Compare these forms of the inequalities with their graphs. Explain how these forms help you determine which region should be shaded.

C Consider the inequality $y < 3x + 6$.

　1. Does the pair (2, 12) satisfy the inequality? Explain.

　2. At the right is the graph of $y < 3x + 6$. How is this graph different from the graphs in Question A? What is the reason for this difference?

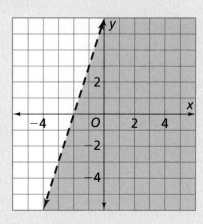

A C E Homework starts on page 72.

4.4 Miles of Emissions
Systems of Linear Inequalities

Jarod's family determines that, on average, they drive their SUV more than twice as many miles as they drive their car. Jarod writes the inequality $s > 2c$, where s represents the number of miles they drive the SUV, and c represents the number of miles they drive the car.

The family agrees to limit the total CO_2 emissions to less than 600 pounds per month. Recalling that the car emits 0.75 pounds of CO_2 per mile and the SUV emits 1.25 pounds of CO_2 per mile, Jarod writes the inequality $0.75c + 1.25s < 600$.

Together, the two inequalities form a **system of linear inequalities.**

$$\begin{cases} s > 2c \\ 0.75c + 1.25s < 600 \end{cases}$$

- What pairs (c, s) are solutions of both inequalities in the system?

Use what you have learned about solving linear inequalities with two variables to develop a strategy for solving systems of inequalities.

Problem 4.4

Ⓐ **1.** Why is the system of two inequalities above an accurate model of the conditions that Jarod's family wants to satisfy?

2. How would the system change if Jarod's family agrees to total emissions that are at most 600 pounds rather than less than 600 pounds?

Ⓑ **1.** Graph the inequalities $0.75c + 1.25s < 600$ and $s > 2c$ on the same coordinate grid.

2. Where on the graph are the points that satisfy both conditions? Find three solution pairs (c, s) for the system. Can Jarod's family drive a total of 800 miles under these conditions?

Problem 4.4 continued

C Adsila's family has a car and an SUV that emit the same amount of CO_2 as the vehicles Jarod's family drives. Adsila's family drives the car *at least* three times as much as the SUV. They want to limit total CO_2 emissions to at most 400 pounds per month. Adsila draws the following graph to see how they can reach their goal.

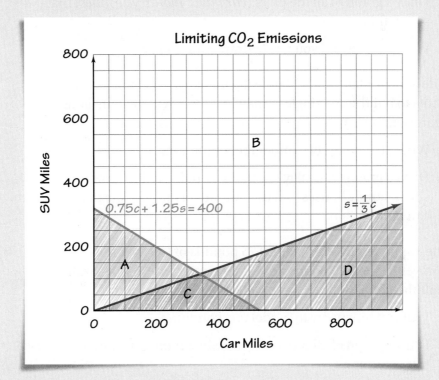

Limiting CO_2 Emissions

$0.75c + 1.25s = 400$

$s = \frac{1}{3}c$

SUV Miles

Car Miles

1. Describe the information that the points in Regions A, B, C, and D represent in terms of the situation.

2. In which region(s) are the points that satisfy both conditions?

A C E Homework starts on page 72.

Applications

1. Ana has a car and a motorcycle. She wants to limit the combined mileage of the two vehicles to at most 500 miles per month.

   a. Write an inequality to model this condition.

   b. Draw a graph of all the pairs (*car miles, motorcycle miles*) that satisfy this condition.

   c. What strategy did you use to draw your graph?

2. A developer plans to build housing for at least 50 families. He wants to build some single-family houses and some four-family apartment buildings.

   a. Write an inequality to model this situation.

   b. Draw a graph to display the possible pairs of the number of single-family houses and the number of apartments the developer can build.

3. The Simon family's car emits 0.75 pounds of CO_2 per mile. Their minivan emits 1.25 pounds of CO_2 per mile. The Simons want to limit their emissions to at most 400 pounds per month.

   a. Write an inequality to model this condition.

   b. Draw a graph of all the pairs (*car miles, minivan miles*) that satisfy this condition.

4. Math Club members are selling games and puzzles. They make a profit of $10 per game and $8 per puzzle. They would like to make a profit of at least $200.

   a. What are some possibilities for the number of games and the number of puzzles the Math Club can sell to reach its goal?

   b. Write an inequality to model this situation.

   c. Draw a graph of all the pairs (*number of games, number of puzzles*) that meet the goal.

For Exercises 5–7, find three pairs (x, y) that satisfy the inequality and three pairs (x, y) that do not. Then, draw a graph showing all the solutions.

5. $x - 4y \geq 8$ **6.** $4x - y \leq 8$ **7.** $x - 4y < 8$

8. For parts (a)–(d), graph the inequality.

    a. $x \geq 8 + 4y$ **b.** $x \geq 4$

    c. $y \leq -2$ **d.** $2x - 4y \geq 8$

9. Math Club members want to advertise their fundraiser each week in the school paper. They know that a front-page ad is more effective than an ad inside the paper. They have a $30 advertising budget. It costs $2 for each front-page ad and $1 for each inside-page ad. The club wants to advertise at least 20 times.

    a. What are some possibilities for the number of front-page ads and the number of inside-page ads the club can place?

    b. Write a system of linear inequalities to model this situation.

    c. Graph your system of inequalities. Be sure it is clear which region shows the solution.

10. The Science Club can spend at most $400 on a field trip to a dinosaur exhibit. It has enough chaperones to allow at most 100 students to go on the trip.

    a. How many students 12 years and under can go on the trip if no students over 12 years go?

    b. How many students over 12 years can go on the trip if no students 12 years or under go?

    c. Write a system of linear inequalities to model this situation.

    d. Graph your system of inequalities. Be sure it is clear which region shows the solution.

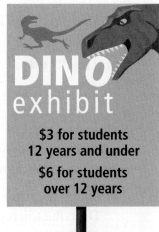

$3 for students
12 years and under

$6 for students
over 12 years

Find three pairs (x, y) that satisfy the system of inequalities and three pairs (x, y) that do not. Then, draw a graph showing all the solutions.

11. $\begin{cases} 4x + 6y \leq 24 \\ x + 5y \leq 10 \end{cases}$ **12.** $\begin{cases} 2x - y \leq 4 \\ -x + y > -1 \end{cases}$

Connections

For Exercises 13 and 14, use a graph to estimate the solution of the system of equations. Check the estimated solution and revise your answer if necessary.

13. $\begin{cases} x + y = 18 \\ 3x - y = 10 \end{cases}$ **14.** $\begin{cases} 80x + 40y = 400 \\ 20x + 80y = 420 \end{cases}$

15. Multiple Choice What is the greatest whole-number value of x for which $4x < 14$?

     A. 3   **B.** 4   **C.** 11   **D.** 14

16. The parks commission in the town of Euclid decides to build a triangular park with one side that is 400 feet long.

     a. What are some possibilities for the lengths of the other sides? Explain.

     b. The city planner wrote these inequalities.

$$x + y > 400 \qquad x + 400 > y \qquad y + 400 > x$$

The variables x and y represent possible lengths for the other two sides of the triangle. Why do these inequalities make sense? Why does the planner need all three inequalities to describe the situation?

     c. Graph the three inequalities from part (b) on the same grid. Describe the region that represents all the possible lengths for the other sides of the park.

     d. Give a pair of lengths for the other two sides of the park. Explain how to find this answer by using your graph from part (c).

     e. Give a possible pair of lengths that could *not* be the other two side lengths. Explain how to find this answer using your graph from part (c).

17. Robin wants to make a smoothie out of milk, strawberry yogurt, and ice. She finds this nutritional information:

Robin wants her smoothie to have about 335 Calories and 24 grams of protein.

a. Write a system of equations to model the conditions for Robin's smoothie.

b. Graph the equations from part (a).

c. How much yogurt and milk should Robin use to make her smoothie? Explain.

18. Kadian also wants a milk-and-yogurt smoothie. She uses the nutritional information from Exercise 17. She wants her smoothie to have at most 400 Calories and at least 20 grams of protein.

a. Write a system of inequalities to model the conditions for Kadian's smoothie.

b. Graph the system of inequalities. Be sure it is clear which region shows the solution.

c. Use your graph from part (b) to describe some combinations of milk and yogurt amounts Kadian could use for her smoothie.

Extensions

19. Carolina wants to make a smoothie out of milk, strawberry yogurt, and ice. She uses the following nutritional information:

She wants her smoothie to have at most 400 Calories, at least 20 grams of protein, and at least 700 milligrams of calcium.

a. Write a system of inequalities to model the conditions for Carolina's smoothie.

b. Graph the system of inequalities. Be sure it is clear which region shows the solution.

c. What are some combinations (*milk, yogurt*) Carolina might choose?

20. Suppose you are making a smoothie. What nutrients are important to you? Would you like your smoothie to be a good source of vitamin C, calcium, fiber, protein, or Calories? What ingredients would you like in your smoothie? Write guidelines for your smoothie. Use nutritional information about the ingredients from a reliable source. Then write a system of inequalities to help you decide how much of each ingredient to include.

In this Investigation, you explored situations that could be modeled with linear inequalities involving two variables. You also solved systems of linear inequalities to find values that satisfied several conditions. The following questions will help you to summarize what you have learned.

Think about these questions. Discuss your ideas with other students and your teacher. Then write a summary of your findings in your notebook.

1. Suppose you are given one linear inequality with two variables. **How** could you use a graph to find solutions of the inequality?

2. Suppose you were given a system of two linear inequalities. **How** could you use a graph to find solutions of the system?

Common Core Mathematical Practices

As you worked on the Problems in this Investigation, you used prior knowledge to make sense of them. You also applied Mathematical Practices to solve the Problems. Think back over your work, the ways you thought about the Problems, and how you used Mathematical Practices.

Jayden described his thoughts in the following way:

In our group, Jen and Nick had a suggestion for solving a system of linear inequalities in Problem 4.4. They said that you could combine the methods we used for solving a system of linear equations and solving a linear inequality.

We graphed the equation of the line associated with each inequality. Then, we found the regions that satisfied both inequalities.

....

Common Core Standards for Mathematical Practice
MP2 Reason abstractly and quantitatively.

• What other Mathematical Practices can you identify in Jayden's reasoning?

• Describe a Mathematical Practice that you and your classmates used to solve a different Problem in this Investigation.

In this Unit, you extended your ability to use algebraic equations and inequalities to solve problems. In particular, you learned how to solve systems of linear equations and inequalities.

Use Your Understanding: Systems

Check your understanding of concepts and methods for solving systems of equations and inequalities by solving the following problems.

1. To encourage attendance to Talent Night, a school offers discounted tickets to students wearing school colors. In all, 250 tickets are sold for a total of $2,100.

Talent Night Tickets

Full Price: $9
Discounted: $6

  a. Let x represent the number of full-price tickets sold. Let y represent the number of discounted tickets sold. Write a system of equations to represent the information about the ticket sales.

  b. Solve the system of equations in two ways.

   • Use a graph to estimate.

   • Use the combination method.

2. The Pep Club sells popcorn and juice at basketball games. The club earns $1.20 for each bag of popcorn and $.80 for each cup of juice.

    a. The club's goal is to earn at least $50 at each game. Let x represent the number of bags of popcorn sold. Let y represent the number of cups of juice sold. Write an inequality to represent the club's goal.

    b. Find at least five pairs (x, y) that satisfy the inequality in part (a). Sketch a graph that represents all the solutions.

    c. The club must buy supplies. They spend $.15 for each bag and $.20 for each cup. Suppose the club can spend at most $15 on supplies for each game. Write an inequality for this constraint.

    d. Find at least five pairs (x, y) that satisfy the inequality in part (c). Sketch a graph of the inequality on the same grid you used in part (b). Label the region that shows the pairs (x, y) that satisfy both constraints.

Explain Your Reasoning

In this Unit, you used graphs and symbolic reasoning to solve systems of equations and inequalities.

3. Consider systems of linear equations in the form $\begin{cases} Ax + By = C \\ Dx + Ey = F \end{cases}$.

    a. Describe the solution of each equation as it is represented on a graph.

    b. Describe the solution of the system as it is represented on a graph.

    c. What numbers of solutions are possible for a system in this form? How are these possibilities shown by the graphs?

    d. How can you solve such a system by using the combination method?

    e. How can you check the solution of a system?

4. Describe the solution graph for each type of inequality.

    a. an inequality with one variable in the form $Ax + B < C$

    b. an inequality with two variables in the form $Ax + By < C$

    c. a system of linear inequalities with two variables in the form
$$\begin{cases} Ax + By < C \\ Dx + Ey < F \end{cases}$$

C **chord** A line segment with endpoints on a circle. Segments *CD* and *AB* in the diagram below are chords.

cuerda Segmento de recta cuyos extremos están sobre un círculo. Los segmentos *CD* y *AB* en el diagrama de abajo son cuerdas.

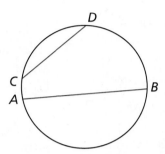

circle A geometric figure consisting of all points *P* that are a fixed distance *r* from a point *C*, called the center of the circle.

círculo Figura geométrica en la que todos los puntos *P* están a una distancia fija *r* de un punto *C*, llamado el centro del círculo.

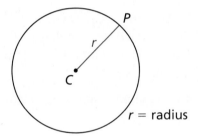

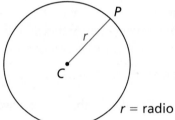

compare Academic Vocabulary
To tell or show how two things are alike and different.

related terms *analyze, relate*

sample Compare the slopes of the lines $-6x + y = 12$ and $2y = 12x + 3$.

> I can write the equations of both lines in slope-intercept form to find their slopes.
>
> $-6x + y = 12$ $2y = 12x + 3$
>
> $y = 6x + 12$ $y = 6x + \dfrac{3}{2}$
>
> The slopes are equal. The lines are parallel since they have the same slope but a different y-intercept.

comparar Vocabulario académico
Decir o mostrar en qué se parecen y en qué se diferencian dos cosas.

términos relacionados *analizar, relacionar*

ejemplo Compara las pendientes de las rectas $-6x + y = 12$ y $2y = 12x + 3$.

> Puedo escribir las ecuaciones de ambas rectas en la forma pendiente-intercepto para hallar sus pendientes.
>
> $-6x + y = 12$ $2y = 12x + 3$
>
> $y = 6x + 12$ $y = 6x + \dfrac{3}{2}$
>
> Las pendientes son iguales. Las rectas son paralelas puesto que tienen la misma pendiente, pero un intercepto en y diferente.

- -

D **decide** Academic Vocabulary
To use the given information and related facts to find a value or make a determination.

related terms *determine, find, conclude*

sample Decide whether to use a graph or the combination method to solve the system. Then solve the system.
$$\begin{cases} x - y = 8 \\ 3x + y = 4 \end{cases}$$

> The coefficients of y in the two equations are opposites, so the combination method is a good method.
>
> $(x - y) + (3x + y) = 8 + 4$
>
> $4x = 12$
>
> $x = 3$
>
> $x - y = 8$
>
> $3 - y = 8$
>
> $-y = 5$
>
> $y = -5$
>
> The solution to the system is $(3, -5)$.

decidir Vocabulario académico
Usar la información dada y los datos relacionados para hallar un valor o tomar una determinación.

términos relacionados *determinar, hallar, concluir*

ejemplo Decide si debes usar una gráfica o el método de combinación para resolver el sistema. Luego, resuelve el sistema.
$$\begin{cases} x - y = 8 \\ 3x + y = 4 \end{cases}$$

> Los coeficientes de y en las dos ecuaciones son opuestos, así que el método de combinación es un buen método.
>
> $(x - y) + (3x + y) = 8 + 4$
>
> $4x = 12$
>
> $x = 3$
>
> $x - y = 8$
>
> $3 - y = 8$
>
> $-y = 5$
>
> $y = -5$
>
> La solución del sistema es $(3, -5)$.

E

explain Academic Vocabulary

To give facts and details that make an idea easier to understand. Explaining can involve a written summary supported by a diagram, chart, table, or a combination of these.

related terms *analyze, clarify, describe, justify, tell*

sample What is the length of segment *OP*? Explain your reasoning.

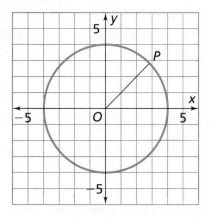

Segment *OP* is a radius of the circle because it connects the center of the circle to a point on the circle. The center of the circle is at the origin and the point (4, 0) lies on the circle. So, the length of the radius is 4 units. Since the lengths of all radii of a given circle are equal, segment *OP* is also 4 units in length.

explicar Vocabulario académico

Proporcionar datos y detalles que hagan que una idea sea más fácil de comprender. Explicar puede incluir un resumen escrito apoyado por un diagrama, una gráfica, una tabla o una combinación de estos.

términos relacionados *analizar, aclarar, describir, justificar, decir*

ejemplo ¿Cuál es la longitud del segmento *OP*? Explica tu razonamiento.

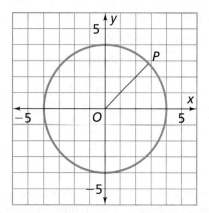

El segmento *OP* es un radio del círculo porque conecta el centro del círculo con un punto en el círculo. El centro del círculo está en el origen y el punto (4, 0) se encuentra en el círculo. Así que la longitud del radio es de 4 unidades. Puesto que las longitudes de todos los radios de un círculo dado son iguales, segmento *OP* tambien tiene 4 unidades de longitud.

English / Spanish Glossary

F

feasible points The set of all solutions that satisfy an equation, an inequality, or a system.

puntos factibles El conjunto de todas las soluciones que satisfacen una ecuación, una desigualdad o un sistema.

identify Academic Vocabulary
To match a definition or a description to an object or to recognize something and be able to name it.

related terms *name, find, classify*

sample Identify the y-intercept of the line $4x - 2y = 10$.

I can find the y-intercept of the line
by setting x = 0 and solving for y.
$$4x - 2y = 10$$
$$4(0) - 2y = 10$$
$$-2y = 10$$
$$y = -5$$
The y-intercept of the line is -5.

identificar Vocabulario académico
Relacionar una definición o una descripción con un objeto, o bien, reconocer algo y ser capaz de nombrarlo.

términos relacionados *nombrar, hallar, clasificar*

ejemplo Identifica el intercepto en y de la recta $4x - 2y = 10$.

Puedo hallar el intercepto en y de la
recta estableciendo que x = 0 y hallando
el valor de y.
$$4x - 2y = 10$$
$$4(0) - 2y = 10$$
$$-2y = 10$$
$$y = -5$$
El intercepto en y de la recta es -5.

linear equation in slope-intercept form The slope-intercept form of a linear equation is $y = mx + b$, where m is the slope and b is the y-intercept.

ecuación lineal en forma pendiente-intercepto La forma pendiente-intercepto de una ecuación lineal es $y = mx + b$, donde m es la pendiente y b es el intercepto en y.

linear equation in standard form The standard form of a linear equation is $Ax + By = C$, where A, B, and C are integers and A and B are not both zero. The equation $6x + 3y = 12$ is in standard form. Although the slope-intercept form, $y = mx + b$, is common and useful, it is not considered the "standard form."

ecuación lineal en forma estándar La forma estándar de una ecuación lineal es $Ax + By = C$, donde A, B, y C son enteros y A y B son distintos de cero. La ecuación $6x + 3y = 12$ está en forma estándar. Aunque la forma pendiente-intercepto, $y = mx + b$, es común y útil, no se considera como la "forma estándar."

linear function A function whose graph is a line.

función lineal Una función cuya gráfica es una recta.

linear inequality A mathematical sentence, such as $Ax + By + C < Dx + Ey + F$, which expresses a relationship of inequality between two quantities, each of which is a linear expression. For example, $y < -2x + 4$ and $6x + 3y \geq 12$ are linear inequalities, as are $x < 3$ and $2x + 3 < 7x$.

desigualdad lineal Un enunciado matemático, como $Ax + By + C < Dx + Ey + F$, que expresa una relación de desigualdad entre dos cantidades, cada una de las cuales es una expresión lineal. Por ejemplo, $y < -2x + 4$ y $6x + 3y \geq 12$ son desigualdades lineales, como también lo son $x < 3$ y $2x + 3 < 7x$.

S

solution of the system A set of values for the variables that makes all the equations or inequalities true.

solución del sistema Un conjunto de valores para las variables que hace que todas las ecuaciones o desigualdades sean verdaderas.

system of linear equations Two or more linear equations that represent constraints on the variables used. A solution of a system of equations is a pair of values that satisfies all the equations in the system. For example, the ordered pair (1, 2) is the solution of the system because it satisfies both equations.

$$\begin{cases} 6x + 3y = 12 \\ -2x + y = 0 \end{cases}$$

sistema de ecuaciones lineales Dos o más ecuaciones lineales que representan limitaciones en las variables usadas. La solución de un sistema de ecuaciones es un par de valores que satisface todas las ecuaciones del sistema. Por ejemplo, el par ordenado (1, 2) es la solución del sistema porque satisface ambas ecuaciones.

$$\begin{cases} 6x + 3y = 12 \\ -2x + y = 0 \end{cases}$$

system of linear inequalities Two or more linear inequalities that represent constraints on the variables used. A solution of a system of inequalities is a pair of values that satisfies all the inequalities in the system. The solution of the system

$$\begin{cases} 6x + 3y < 12 \\ -2x + y > 0 \end{cases}$$

is indicated by region A in the graph below. All the points in this region satisfy *both* inequalities. The points in region B satisfy $-2x + y > 0$, but *not* $6x + 3y < 12$. The points in region C satisfy $6x + 3y < 12$, but *not* $-2x + y > 0$. The points in the unshaded region do not satisfy either inequality.

sistema de desigualdades lineales Dos o más desigualdades lineales que representan limitaciones en las variables usadas. La solución de un sistema de desigualdades es un par de valores que satisface todas las desigualdades en el sistema. La solución del sistema

$$\begin{cases} 6x + 3y < 12 \\ -2x + y > 0 \end{cases}$$

está indicada por la región A en la gráfica de abajo. Todos los puntos de esta región satisfacen *ambas* desigualdades. Los puntos de la región B satisfacen $-2x + y > 0$, pero *no* $6x + 3y < 12$. Los puntos de la región C satisfacen $6x + 3y < 12$, pero *no* $-2x + y > 0$. Los puntos de la región sin sombrear no satisfacen ninguna desigualdad.

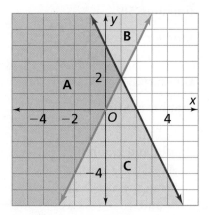

Index

Acknowledgments

Cover Design

Three Communication Design, Chicago

Photographs

Photo locators denoted as follows: Top (T), Center (C), Bottom (B), Left (L), Right (R), Background (Bkgd)

003 VisionsofAmerica/Joe Sohm/Digital Vision/Getty Images.